KU-480-740

Reflective Practice in Social Work

SECOND EDITION

Edited by
CHRISTINE KNOTT
and
TERRY SCRAGG

Series Editors: Jonathan Parker and Greta Bradley

LearningMatters

MERTHYR TYDFIL COLLEGE
LIBRARY

First published in 2007 by Learning Matters Ltd
Second edition published in 2010

All rights reserved. No part of this publication may be reproduced, stored in a retrieval system, or transmitted in any form or by any means, electronic, mechanical, photocopying, recording, or otherwise, without prior permission in writing from Learning Matters.

© 2010 Introduction Christine Knott and Terry Scragg, Chapter 1 Christine Knott, Chapter 2 Christine Knott and Jan Spafford, Chapter 3 Gill Butler, Chapter 4 Gill Constable, Chapter 5 Andy Mantell, Chapter 6 Sandra Wallis, Chapter 7 Chris Smethurst, Chapter 8 Carleton Edwards, Chapter 9 Terry Scragg, Chapter 10 Janet McCray, Conclusion Christine Knott and Terry Scragg

British Library Cataloguing in Publication Data
A CIP record for this book is available from the British Library

ISBN 978 1 84445 364 1

The right of Christine Knott, Terry Scragg, Jan Spafford, Gill Butler, Gill Constable, Andy Mantell, Sandra Wallis, Chris Smethurst, Carleton Edwards and Janet McCray to be identified as the Authors of this Work has been asserted by them in accordance with the Copyright, Designs and Patents Act 1988.

Cover and text design by Code 5 Design Associates Ltd
Project Management by Deer Park Productions, Tavistock, Devon
Typeset by Pantek Arts Ltd, Maidstone, Kent
Printed and bound in Great Britain by Bell & Bain Ltd, Glasgow

Learning Matters Ltd
33 Southernhay East
Exeter EX1 1NX
Tel: 01392 215560
info@learningmatters.co.uk
www.learningmatters.co.uk

Contents

Editors and contributors

The following are all current or former members of the Social Work Subject Area, University of Chichester, with the exception of Carleton Edwards:

Gill Butler is Deputy Dean Social Work Subject Area

Gill Constable is Senior Lecturer in Social Work

Christine Knott (editor) was formerly Head of the Social Work Subject Area

Janet McCray is Principal Lecturer in Health and Social Care Leadership and Management

Andy Mantell is Senior Lecturer in Social Work

Terry Scragg (editor) is a Visiting Fellow and was formerly Principal Lecturer in Management

Jan Spafford was formerly Principal Lecturer (Learning and Teaching)

Chris Smethurst is Senior Lecturer in Social Work

Sandra Wallis is Senior Lecturer in Social Work

Carleton Edwards is Training and Development Manager (Practice Learning), West Sussex Adults' and Children's Services

Acknowledgements

We would like to thank Di Page, Kate Lodge and Jonathan Parker for their help and encouragement throughout the process of preparing this book for publication.

Introduction

This book is written for the student social worker and explores a range of approaches to reflective practice that will be useful across the whole of your programme of study and in subsequent years as you move into practice learning. Experienced and qualified social workers contributing to practice learning will also be able to use this book for consultation, teaching, revision and to gain an insight into the expectations raised by the qualifying degree in social work. Essentially this book is designed to assist you in developing an understanding of the concept of the reflective practitioner, and to learn how, in conjunction with your practice assessor and others, you can take a perspective on your own actions and experiences that have the potential for refining and reframing your practice as a result of these deliberations. Reflection is central to good social work practice, but only if action results from that reflection.

Great emphasis is now placed on developing the skills of reflection about, in and on practice. This has developed over many years in social work, and is not only important during your education to become a social worker; it is considered key to continued professional development. As we move to a profession that acknowledges life-long learning as a way of keeping up-to-date, ensuring that research informs practice and in honing skills and values for practice, it is important to begin the process at the outset of your development. The importance of professional development is clearly shown by its inclusion in the National Occupational Standards and reflected in the General Social Care Council (GSCC) Code of Practice for Employees.

Book structure

This book is written by former and current staff of the School of Social Studies, University of Chichester and a colleague from West Sussex Adults' and Children's Services, where there has been a long history of social work education in partnership with local agencies. As you will see below, the book starts with a broad exploration of reflective practice drawing on some of the key texts that have informed the development of the concept, and some of the processes that can be adopted in reflective practice. This is then used as the basis for the following chapters that are concerned with aspects of the development of the reflective practitioner from a range of standpoints. Finally, we explore issues of the management of social work practice and inter-professional leadership in the context of reflection.

Part 1 What is reflective practice?

Chapter 1 explores what is meant by reflective practice and some of the potential outcomes from using this technique. The chapter then examines the roots of the concept of reflective practice, with the work of Schön as our starting point, and goes on to discuss its application to social work. The terminology around reflective practice will be discussed as will the relationship between evidence-based practice and reflective practice. The chapter also acknowledges that some environmental conditions in organisations may make reflection more difficult, and that the positive relationships and processes need to be in place for constructive reflection to take place.

Chapter 2 examines the methods used to start the process of reflection. These methods will be familiar to most social work and other professional educators. As a social work student you will find this a key part of the process of learning and teaching on your qualifying programme. This chapter will draw on methods that have been discussed in the literature and also practised in both qualifying and post-qualifying social work education. We suggest a wide range of strategies and techniques that you can test out as a way of developing the practical skills of reflection, including how to start the process of reflection and how to maintain a reflective approach as you develop your social work career.

Part 2 Developing the reflective practitioner

Chapter 3 recognises that the reflective process involves the emotions. This chapter questions the apparent tension between reason and emotion and explores some of the difficulties that result from this way of thinking. The role of language in both shaping and reflecting dominant discourses in practice is explored. The importance in social work of understanding and processing emotions is then considered, with particular reference to child protection practice. The concept of emotional intelligence is identified, as providing a helpful framework for developing emotionally competent practice. A series of reflective tasks is provided to support the development of emotional awareness and regulation, which are considered central to the development of emotional intelligence.

Chapter 4 focuses on reflection that leads to challenging self-limiting beliefs and promotes action through the use of an approach underpinned by cognitive behaviour therapy. This theory is explained by the use of case studies, and their application for social work students as well as work with service users and carers. A number of approaches will be considered such as writing reflectively, analysis of self-talk and belief systems and the use of the ABC technique to challenge self-defeating thoughts. The aim of the chapter is to enable you to develop ideas of how you can reflect in a purposeful manner, which will enable you to problem-solve, and develop personal confidence and professional competence.

Chapter 5 highlights the potential pitfalls when applying reflective practice to work with carers. The evolving professional conception of 'the carer' is examined and contrasted with the lived experience of people providing care. Case material will be included from new research with families with a family member with Huntington's Disease. The chapter goes on to reflect on the participation of service users and carers in social work and the challenging perspective they may bring. An exploration of knowledge, experience and power in understanding and interpretation is included and how to use the reflective process to consider other position perspectives and realities.

Social work often involves statutory work with *involuntary* service users, who can be hostile and aggressive. Chapter 6 examines the important role reflective practice can play in these situations as a means of avoiding the risk of social workers reacting in ways that can, albeit unintentionally, actually work to increase the danger for service users and social workers. The process is explained through the concept of professional dangerousness; the chapter provides some useful exercises and concludes with some practical suggestions on how professional dangerousness might be minimised.

Chapter 7 discusses gender in social work, and how the men and woman in social work can be both shaped by socialisation and influenced by others' expectation of gender roles, and what are seen as appropriate behaviours for male and female social workers. The chapter explores theories about masculinity and femininity, and some of the tensions you may experience when exploring gender differences and attempting to apply them in your practice. The chapter provides you with a range of opportunities to explore gender issues, from a personal perspective, in the context of the social work settings and practice situations, and through the use of exercises, case studies and research findings.

Chapter 8 considers reflective practice on placement. Key Role 6 of the National Occupational Standards, the demonstration of professional competence – is central to this process. Reflection on practice, and reflection in practice while on placement, is the focus of this chapter. Supervision by the practice assessor is identified as an important component of this process, and a range of materials and exercises is included. These are intended to assist your development as a social worker, with the beneficial outcome of improving your skills in working with service users and carers, as well as challenging assumptions and preconceptions. The chapter has been written to be mainly of relevance to students, although it will also be of interest to practice assessors and social workers involved in post-qualifying training.

Part 3 Maintaining reflective practice

Chapter 9 introduces you to the world of management, particularly the work of the first line manager and some of the tensions inherent in management roles in social work. The case is made in this chapter for managers maintaining a reflective approach to their practice as managers of the social work service within increasingly managerialist organisations, and similarly encouraging a reflective approach to the work with the social workers they manage. The second part of this chapter explores how students can actively manage their relationship with their line manager in the context of practice learning. Lastly this chapter introduces you to a range of techniques that can be used when reflecting on and about practice.

Finally Chapter 10 discusses how increasingly social work will be practised in an inter-professional context in complex new organisational structures, with leadership in these new structures essential. This chapter explores the application of a reflective tool to support inter-professional leadership. This chapter builds on previous chapters and themes in relation to the overall concept, critically analysing the use of reflective models in the social care arena. It challenges you to explore how critical exploration of your own thought and feeling processes, knowledge and experience can support leadership, prevent professional introspection and bring fresh approaches to problem-solving and change in the inter-professional context.

Learning features

This book is interactive. You are encouraged to work through the book as an active participant, taking responsibility for your learning, in order to increase your knowledge, understanding and ability to apply this learning to practice. You will be expected to reflect creatively on how immediate learning needs can be met in the area of assessment, planning, intervention and review and how your professional learning can be developed in your future career.

Case studies throughout the book will help you to examine theories and models of reflective practice. We have devised activities that require you to reflect on experiences, situations and events and help you to review and summarise learning undertaken. In this way your knowledge will become deeply embedded as part of your development. When you come to practice learning in an agency the work and reflection undertaken here will help you to improve and hone your skills and knowledge.

This book will introduce knowledge and learning activities for you as a student social worker concerning the central processes relating to issues of reflective practice in all areas of the discipline. Suggestions for further reading will be made at the end of each chapter.

Part One

What is reflective practice?

Chapter 1

Reflective practice revisited

Christine Knott

A C H I E V I N G   A   S O C I A L   W O R K   D E G R E E

This chapter will help you meet the following National Occupational Standards for Social Work.
Key Role 6: Demonstrate professional competence in social work practice
- Research, analyse and use current knowledge of best social work practice.
- Work within agreed standards of social work practice and ensure own professional development.

Achieving a post-qualifying social work award
This chapter will also assist you to evidence post-qualifying national criteria at the Specialist level:
(v) Use reflection and critical analysis to continuously develop and improve their specialist practice, including their practice in inter-professional and inter-agency contexts, drawing systematically, accurately and appropriately on theories, models and relevant up-to-date research.
It will also introduce you to the following academic standards as set out in the subject benchmark statement:
3.1.5 Nature of social work practice
- Processes of reflection and evaluation and familiarity with a range of approaches for evaluating welfare outcomes and significance for the development of practice and practitioner.

This introductory chapter revisits previous writing about reflection not just in social work but in allied professions too. The main starting point will be to re-examine the work of Donald Schön and subsequent ideas, including depth learning and reflexive practice. Evidence-based practice is also discussed, not in opposition to reflection but hopefully to propose a more integrated approach to social work practice, which necessarily includes both.

What is reflective practice?

The terms 'reflection', 'reflective practice', 'the reflective practitioner' are very current in social work education and practice at both qualifying and post-qualifying levels and have been for a number of years. You will also find them current in the other professions with which social work collaborates to provide the best service for those people who are users of the service, particularly the health professions (Tate and Sills, 2004). While the idea of reflection sounds easy, it is far from being so and many writers acknowledge the complexity of the concept. Parker and Bradley (2003) state that social work practice is driven by theory, some taken from formal knowledge that you will learn about on your course such as attachment theory and theories relating to loss and bereavement. You will also be introduced to knowledge about how to practise using such methods as task-centred, cognitive-behavioural or person-centred approaches, among others. You will be expected to apply these theories to your practice when you are out on assessed practice or indeed when you are a qualified practitioner. What also happens during and after qualification, according to Parker and Bradley, however, is that you also begin to construct a body of informal knowledge, or experiential wisdom from working with people in practice. Reflection and reflective practice help you to integrate theoretical learning, whether formal or informal, into your practice.

Horner (2004), in exploring the question *What is social work?*, considers reflection to be central to good social work practice but only if action results from that reflection, which is known as reflective practice. He considers that reflecting about, on and in practice needs to be developed during initial social work education and is the key to continuing professional development. Hence it is a concept that will underpin post-qualifying training too. He states that a questioning approach that looks in a critical way at thoughts, experiences and practice and seeks to heighten skills as a result of those deliberations is the hallmark of reflection. This message is reiterated in other books in the Transforming Social Work series. For example, Parker and Bradley (2003) also comment on the need for developing a reflective capability, stating that a thoughtful and planned approach will help to make social work clear to service users and also more open to review, so that practice can be improved in the future. At the University of Chichester reflection and reflective practice have been built into the curriculum of all social work and related professional programmes over many years (Ashford, Blake and Knott, 1998). This occurs in a number of ways, which will be explored particularly in the next chapter.

So what is this phenomenon of reflection?

Most of the public service professions are committed to the development of reflective practice. For example, Rolfe, Freshwater and Jasper (2001) writing about nursing, Tate and Sills (2004) about health professions and Jennings and Kennedy (1996) writing about education are clear that it is relevant for the development of these professions too. Other writers, including Moon (1999, 2004), take a more generic educational approach so that the concept is valid for a range of professional development activities, not least social work teaching in higher education. Moon (2004), concludes that a common-sense definition of reflection is that it is applied to relatively complicated, ill-structured ideas for which there is not an obvious solution and is largely based on the further processing of knowledge and understanding that we already possess. She suggests that the following outcomes can result from reflective processes:

- learning, knowledge and understanding;
- some form of action;
- a process of critical review;
- personal and continuing professional development;
- reflection on the process of learning or personal functioning (meta-cognition);
- the building of theory from observations in practice situations;

- the making of decisions/resolution of uncertainty, the solving of problems, empower-ment and emancipation;

- unexpected outcomes (e.g. images, ideas that could be solutions to dilemmas or seen as creative activity);

- emotion (that can be an outcome or can be part of the process);

- clarification and the recognition that there is a need for further reflection.

(Moon, 2004, p84)

ACTIVITY **1.1**

Think of an interaction that happened recently on your course, either in class or in practice and analyse it from the above list of outcomes. What was the main outcome for you?

Comment

It may be that your reflection centred on either thoughts, feelings or actions. It does not matter which but on a relatively simple level most of us can reflect back to a situation and find some further meaning about it either what we were thinking or feeling or what action resulted.

However, in a thought-provoking social work article, Ixer (1999) makes the case in the title for there being no such thing as reflection. He considers that often uncritical attention has been paid to developing and assessing reflective practice in social work education. He finds definitions of reflection and reflective practice to be problematic and theoretical explanations open to debate. *We do not know enough about reflection or how intricate and complex cognitive processes can enhance learning to be able to assess it fairly. Much of what is assessed remains speculative and conjectural* (Ixer, 1999, p522). In this book we aim to share what we have discovered about the nature of reflection in a number of areas relevant to social work and how reflective practice can be maintained in the ever-changing context in which qualified social workers practice.

Roots of reflective practice

So where has the notion of reflection and reflective practice come from? Writers taking a his-torical approach to the development of ideas on reflective practice generally go back to the work of the educational philosopher, John Dewey, writing in the inter-war period (Dewey, 1933, 1938). His view was that people only begin to reflect when there is a problem to be solved (see Moon above). This is very familiar for social work. Dewey thinks that reflection is the continual re-evaluation of personal beliefs, assumptions and ideas in the light of experi-ence and data and the generation of alternative interpretations of those experiences and data.

The starting point for this revisiting, however, begins later with the work of such adult edu-cationalists as Donald Schön (1983, 1987, 2002) writing about the reflective practitioner and the work of Steven Brookfield (1987) writing about critical thinking and the associated idea of critical learning. Schön advocated two types of reflection, reflection-on-action and reflection-in-action. So first *reflection-on-action* or thinking back on something already done, away from the action, starting with recall and a description of what happened. This is what Activity 1.1 asked you to do. It then moves to a fuller examination of the experience initially using who, what, where, when, why and how type questions. The process therefore aims to transform the experience into knowledge, which is different to just thinking about practice which is merely recall without learning from it.

The idea of the *lens* here may be helpful in trying to understand the experience being reflected upon. What frame of reference (or lens) is being used to make sense of what has happened? What theories are being applied to this situation? It is easy to reinforce previously held opinions about people and situations which may lead to prejudice and discriminatory practice if we do not recognise what we are using to make sense of reflections. It is also important to recognise what we are we feeling as we reflect on the experience. Are the feelings positive or negative? For example, did you feel anxious or confident or satisfied or disappointed? When someone who wears glasses puts them on, the difference in being able to see clearly is immense. Things come into focus and clearer patterns emerge. This is what reflection on action can begin to achieve for the beginning professional practitioner. So it is essentially a retrospective activity, thinking about an event after it has taken place. 'Hindsight is wonderful' is a phrase that is often heard. It can be summarised as a process of transforming experience into knowledge and understanding, rather than a process of skill acquisition. There is clearly a strong cognitive element to this process but there is also a feeling/affective process, which also needs to be included in the reflective process. Remembrance and recognition of feelings that were uppermost are an important element in the reflective process, although the facilitation of such reflection needs to be undertaken sensitively.

ACTIVITY *1.2*

Reflect back to a recent practice experience, either simulated on your course or actual, and describe the lens that you used to make sense of what you observed. What feelings were uppermost for you?

Comment

There are a number of techniques that can be used to enhance this process of reflection-on-action; some involve talking either one-to-one or in a small group, writing, other creative activities, again either on your own, with another or in a group. As social workers we need to become familiar with the process of reflection and you will find it a fundamental process at both qualifying and post-qualifying levels. Learning from experience and by experience is an essential element of social work training both in class and practice. Some of these initiating activities to stimulate reflection will be explored in more detail in the following chapter.

Schön's second type of reflection he calls *reflection-in-action* or thinking about what you are doing while you are doing it, having a 'feel' for something and doing something about it. This way of practising is the more important form of reflection for experienced professional practitioners. It is probably more relevant to qualified social workers undertaking post-qualifying training. This is a model that celebrates the intuitive and artistic approaches that can be applied to uncertain and shifting, swampy situations. Schön (1991) advocates the development of a practice artistry rather than a technical solution to deal with the *indeterminate swampy zones of practice involving uncertainty, uniqueness and value conflict*. This is so familiar to social work practice and is essential if you are to work effectively with the people who use services and the learning that results from effective engagement. It can be considered as an intuitive reflectivity, where thinking and acting go together, as one is practising. Associated with this is the idea of *knowing in action or theories in use*, which describes the knowledge that is shown in practice, which is not described beforehand. The idea of professional artistry as opposed to technical competence is debated below, as it is not without its critics.

Social work and social work education moved into a competence-based approach in the late 1980s with the development of the Diploma in Social Work (Dip SW) and now to a task and function approach with the development of National Occupational Standards (NOS) for the Social Work Degree in 2002. The danger of a technical/rational base for social work practice based on NOS is that it may lead people to think there are certainties in social work when experience tells practitioners otherwise. Nevertheless, National Occupational Standards are now in vogue for all aspects of social work and social care and have also been developed for post-qualifying social work. Other writers would argue that there are swampy lowlands in research too (Taylor and White, 2000, p200).

As well as the lens, by which we make sense of our reflections, mentioned above, this is where the addition of the metaphor of the mirror may be helpful, as the *mirror* reflects back to us what is going on for us in tricky situations. It also helps us to recognise what we are feeling as well as thinking. A good tutor/mentor/practice teacher/assessor as well as fellow students and service users and carers can facilitate this mirroring process, or clear reflecting back. Good feedback can aid learning during an experience as well as afterwards. So it is relevant for reflection-in-action as well as reflection-on-action.

Moon (2004) raises the following interesting discussion points.

- *Emotion* is central to the reflective process.

- *Reflection* is always about 'my own' processes (i.e., always in the first person).

- Some people cannot reflect.

ACTIVITY **1.3**

What do you think about the above points raised by Moon? Are you encouraged to express emotion in your written work? Are you encouraged to write in the first person? Is reflection a universal attribute or is it a learned skill?

Comment

Generally you will be required to write in the third person on your social work pro-grammes. However, we consider it appropriate to use the first person if you are writing reflectively on your own experience. We would expect all social work students to be able to reflect on their practice. To us it is the hallmark of a professional practitioner.

Depth learning

Jenny Moon (2004) has an interesting chapter on the depth quality of reflective learning, which potentially introduces the idea of levels of learning or, in other words, a potential hierarchy of reflection. This seems to be logical so that ways of developing deeper learning and reflection appear to resonate with development in academic terms from first-year undergraduate level to post-qualifying/postgraduate level/master's level. From the adult education literature, deep reflection is associated with Mezirow's (1992) concept of per-spective transformation. It may also resonate with ideas about the development of professional practitioners from novice to expert. The novice is characterised by adherence to taught rules and little discretionary judgement, while the expert is characterised by free-dom from rules and guidelines with an intuitive grasp of situations, based on deep understanding, knowing what is possible, using analytical approaches in novel situations or when new problems occur. Thus the expert stage is characterised by implicit and uncon-scious practice. Interestingly this can also be applied to the competence model of development from unconscious incompetence, to conscious incompetence, to conscious competence and finally to unconscious competence.

Higher education is very familiar with levels with the publication of the Quality Assurance Agency Framework for Higher Education Qualifications (FHEQ) with associated learning outcomes and assessment criteria with which you, as a student, will be only too familiar.

The taxonomy of learning in the cognitive domain is also relevant. So learning goes from knowledge to understanding to application to analysis to synthesis to evaluation. A more gender-based approach on the development of knowledge is that of Belenky, Clinchy, Golberger and Tartule (1987), which goes from silence to constructed knowledge. The meta-cognitive process is therefore supported by models of learning, which facilitate the reflective process. When it comes to practice, fewer models of taxonomy or hierarchical nature exist, although in social care different kinds of practitioner and the training they need have emerged, led by Skills for Care and the Children's Workforce Development Council (CWDC). The National Occupational Standards for Social Work apply whatever the level of cognitive learning. Whether you are on an undergraduate, postgraduate or master's level qualifying programme, the NOS have all to be met to the same level of practice capability.

Evidence-based practice and reflective practice

Another term that is commonly used in professional social work education is 'evidence-based practice'. It may be that your university course favours one approach above the other, as they can be argued to be in opposition to each other, as in their most extreme forms they foster entirely different ways of developing and using theory in practice (Healy, 2005, p97). Evidence-based practice relies on rational knowledge to inform practice that has been tested through scientific methods. In Schön's language it is technical/rational rather than intuitive artistry. It may be entitled 'empirical practice' (Reid, 1994). Healy argues that it is probably better to think about evidence-based practice and reflective practice as a continuum rather than as an opposition. The social work professional needs to be able to articulate the effectiveness of proposed interventions, or ways of working with people who use services, based on empirical research. This is particularly so where difficult judgements are being made, for example in work involving safeguarding children and mental health.

The evidence-based approach is to be found in other professions, particularly in the health and criminal justice arenas. So as multi-professional work is increasingly advocated it is important that social workers in training recognise and value the approach from which other colleagues may be operating. Increasingly employing organisations, both statutory and independent, service users and carers and the general public want to be clear on what basis decisions are made.

Healy (2005) argues that evidence-based practice is essentially a top-down approach to theory development and its application. In other words social workers are the subject and users of knowledge, not the makers of it. The separation of knowledge development from its application in practice means that social workers do not have the time or the scientific tools to develop robust theories of practice and have little opportunity to question how the knowledge was developed or how it might be challenged in practice. By contrast, the reflective approach recognises the value of the practitioner's lived experience of practice as a basis for making and using knowledge in practice. It respects the specificity of each service user's unique situation. Social work is a messy occupation, which involves perceptions and feelings as well as material facts (Parton, 2001). However, reflective practice, which uses the social worker's reflections as the basis of knowledge creation and use, is also problematic. The emphasis on tacit or intuitive knowledge above knowledge from an evidence base means that it will be inaccessible to other colleagues, service users and carers, employers and funding agencies. So both approaches are open to criticism. This may lead to confusion for social workers in training too. The view that is taken at Chichester is that both approaches are valuable but some integration is necessary. You need to be clear where the information informing your practice comes from. If it is purely based on your own subjective reflections, then it needs to be informed by evidence. A question frequently asked both verbally and on written work is: *What is your evidence for that?* If the information is only based on evidence from research then you will be asked to reflect on the research and find meaning relevant to yourself and the practice situation. Thus we promote the concept of the informed reflective practitioner.

What is reflexive practice?

Taylor and White (2000, p206) define reflexivity as:

> *an elusive term often used interchangeably with reflection. It encompasses reflection but also incorporates other features so that it is not just the individualised action of*

separate practitioners in the manner suggested by reflective practice; rather it is the collective action of an academic discipline or occupational group. For workers in health and welfare it means that they subject knowledge claims and practice to analysis.

So it could be argued that reflexive practice is just another way of describing practice that is more like Schön's reflection-in-action but generally reflexion is not just concerned with an interior individualistic humanistic process but involves iteration with exterior social and political processes. This of course is the essential differentiating element of social work from the other professions. Social workers 'work the social' (Parton, 2001). Reflection of itself does not lead to 'good enough' professional practice. It needs to be tested against agreed standards for that profession. In the case of social work this standard is now enshrined in the General Social Care Council's (GSCC) Codes of Practice (GSCC, 2002). It could equally be argued that having a code of ethics does not of itself lead to ethical practice. Indeed those social workers involved in statutory social work have to deal with many ethical issues arising from the increasingly bureaucratic, managerial context in which they are required to practise. The role of the state has changed from one of provider of welfare to vulnerable people to one of commissioner and regulator. The case could be made that the needs of managers are privileged over the needs of service users and carers. The reflective practitioner therefore needs to be able to place their reflections-on-and-in-action in the social arena of social policy and economics.

Critical thinking

The term *critical* also appears to be important, so that reflection needs to be critical, involving critical thinking and critical self-awareness and leading to ethical practice.

According to Paul and Elder (2005) of the Foundation for Critical Thinking, a critical thinker is capable of:

- *raising* vital questions and problems, clearly and precisely;
- *gathering* and assessing relevant information, using theories and ideas to interpret it effectively;
- *reaching* conclusions and solutions, tested against relevant criteria;
- *thinking* open-mindedly, owning assumptions and consequences;
- *communicating* effectively.

Brown and Rutter (2006) in their book on critical thinking for social work explore the intellectual resources needed for critical thinking as follows:

- background knowledge;
- critical concepts;
- critical thinking standards;
- strategies;
- habits of mind.

A simpler way of expressing this is in Smith's (1992) three key factors of knowledge, authority and willingness to doubt.

Brown and Rutter argue that *the skills of critical thinking allow the best quality decisions or actions possible for the situations we encounter* (Brown and Rutter, 2006, p10). This capability is definitely needed in social work practice.

Ethical issues

The other aspect that seems to be involved in developing the critical reflective practitioner is the awareness of ethical issues or value conflicts and the potential, as there is in any relationship or process, for oppression. Taylor (1995) writing about facilitating public/private reflection recognises that it can generate difficult feelings with painful personal experiences being reactivated. Brown and Rutter (2006) make a similar point that the process of critical thinking can be threatening, provoke anxiety and create adverse reactions from other people. They advise people to seek support if the negative aspects are adversely affecting them. This applies to the educational setting as well as the practice setting. So the process of critical thinking and thus critical reflection needs support. This is where a tutor in the educational setting and a practice teacher/supervisor in the practice setting are crucial. If this support is not forthcoming then there is the ethical question as to the level to which critical reflection should be encouraged. Recognition of feelings therefore is an important part of critical reflection. There is some evidence that men find it harder to engage in reflection than women (Moon, 2004, p93). Gender and social work will be discussed further in Chapter 7.

All experiential learning has an element of risk as the responsibility for the level of engagement passes from the tutor/mentor to the students in learning environments and from the practice teacher/assessor in the practice environment. Guidance should be given about the potential for distress, either from the nature of the material reflected upon or the actual process of reflection.

Ixer (1999) makes the important point that:

> Social work has become steeped in demands that students should demonstrate reflection in practice as a learning outcome. The danger this poses to vulnerable learners in the assessment relationship, when assessors' own conceptions of reflection may be poorly formed and may not match those of their students, is worryingly likely to compound the imbalance of power between them … . Until such time as we can state more clearly what it is we have to accept that there is no theory of reflection that can be adequately assessed. (p513)

In a recent article Yip (2006) strikes a note of caution and about self-reflection in reflective practice. Yip agrees that under appropriate conditions reflection can be constructive and result in self-enhancement. However, the pertinent point is made that under inappropriate conditions it can be highly destructive to a social worker's self-development. The inappropriate conditions may include such things as an oppressive social environment at work/placement which could include a highly critical supervisor, apathetic colleagues, a demanding working environment, which includes a demanding workload. The development of a trusting relationship with the practice assessor and the supervisor in the workplace is essential for reflection to take place honestly and openly so that learning and professional practice are enhanced. Disclosure of learning needs and practice difficulties must not be misused so that the student/worker feels undermined and/or exploited. As stated above, reflection is a powerful process and requires mutual respect by all parties. Perhaps more seriously, reflection may uncover unresolved past traumas from childhood, family and partner relationships. Under these circumstances, where physical and mental health issues are apparent, Yip argues that self-reflection in reflective practice may create more harm than good. The clear message is that appropriate conditions need to be in place for constructive reflection to take place.

This book is attempting to add to that clarification so that both the process and outcome of reflection can be more clearly taught and assessed.

CHAPTER SUMMARY

There is no doubt that the terminology around reflection, reflexivity and reflective practice is difficult and that some educators and practitioners will favour one interpretation above another. We would argue that an integration of both the reflective and evidence-based approaches to learning and practice are needed and that they are not necessarily mutually exclusive. Social workers need to be *informed reflective practitioners*. They need to know from research which interventions are most likely to lead to the best outcomes. In other words, 'what works' but not to be limited by that as social work research is relatively in its infancy and some of it is contradictory. The establishment of the Social Care Institute for Excellence (SCIE) was a move in the right direction for the recognition and funding of social work and social care research and its dissemination. The aim of the SCIE is to improve the experience of people who use social care services by developing and promoting knowledge about good practice in social care. The establishment of the Social Work Task Force in 2008 recognised that social work faces acute challenges and concerns, not least the status of the profession as a whole. It will report to the Department of Health and the Department for Children, Schools and Families and make recommendations about high quality practice. Social workers will need to continually develop their capacity for reflection so that they are aware of what sort of practitioner they are and how effective they are in their practice. Supervisors and managers need to create an appropriate environment in which reflection can occur to good effect.

FURTHER READING

The following books provide essential information about reflective practice.

Healy, K (2005) *Social work theories in context: Creating frameworks for practice.* Basingstoke: Palgrave Macmillan.

Moon, J (1999) *Reflection in learning and professional development: Theory and practice.* London: Kogan Page.

Schön, D (2002) From technical rationality to reflection-in-action. In R Harrison, F Reeve, A Hanson and J Clarke (eds) *Supporting lifelong learning. Volume One. Perspectives on learning.* London: Routledge/Open University Press.

Yip, K (2006) Self-reflection in reflective practice: A note of caution. *British Journal of Social Work*, 36, 777–88.

Chapter 2
Getting started

Christine Knott and Jan Spafford

A C H I E V I N G   A   S O C I A L   W O R K   D E G R E E

This chapter will help you meet the following National Occupational Standards for Social Work.
Key Role 6: Demonstrate professional competence in social work practice
- Research, analyse and use current knowledge of best social work practice.
- Work within agreed standards of social work practice and ensure own professional development.

Achieving a post-qualifying social work award
This chapter will also assist you to evidence post-qualifying national criteria at the Specialist level:
(v) Use reflection and critical analysis to continuously develop and improve their specialist practice, including their practice in inter-professional and inter-agency contexts, drawing systematically, accurately and appropriately on theories, models and relevant up-to-date research.

It will also introduce you to the following academic standards as set out in the subject benchmark statement:
3.1.5 Nature of social work practice
- Processes of reflection and evaluation and familiarity with a range of approaches for evaluating welfare outcomes and significance for the development of practice and practitioner.

This chapter links with the previous chapter and offers some useful and practical ways to develop your skills of reflection. Most social work courses at qualifying and post-qualifying levels will require you to complete reflective pieces of work, which will be assessed. Some may form part of your assessment of the professional practice elements of your course and others will be part of your learning and assessment of university-based elements. Many students find this process of reflection difficult to grasp but once the process has been developed it will underpin your learning about the theory and practice of social work while you are a student and on into your life as a qualified social worker. So the earlier you address and value the process of reflection the better. It will also underpin your continuing professional development (CPD) as a social worker, which is now a requirement for continuing registration with the GSCC. If you continue into post-qualifying studies you will also be required to enhance your reflective capabilities. In terms of inter-professional work most other professions with whom you will work such as the health professions and teaching also value the process of reflection as part of their professional and post-professional education and training.

The framework for this chapter starts with understanding how we learn and some models of learning from experience. If, as according to Thompson (2002), the reflective practitioner is a worker who is able to use experience and theoretical perspectives to guide and inform practice, then that is what they need to experience on their qualifying course. Reflective practice involves being able to apply theory to practice, drawing on existing frameworks of ideas and knowledge so that you do not have to reinvent the wheel for each new situation as it arises but also being beware of 'ready made solutions' (Thompson, 2002, p222).

Getting started on any activity is for some of us the hardest part. However, once we have got going we wonder what all the fuss was about. The avoidance of getting started is known as displacement activity. Instead of getting on with the required activity we do all sorts of other things, like having a cup of coffee, putting a load into the washing machine and then having another cup of coffee and so on. We call it the 'I'll just' syndrome. We say to ourselves 'I'll just take the dog for a walk' or 'I'll just do the washing', etc. Extreme displacement can find us doing those things that we would avoid doing in normal circumstances, such as cleaning the oven or sorting out the mess in the garage. We can all experience blocks to reflection and so to learning. A useful early activity is to reflect on experiences that have enhanced or blocked learning.

ACTIVITY 2.1

Make a list of three good and three poor learning experiences. What happened that helped your learning and what happened that blocked your learning? Where possible share the results of this activity with a colleague on the course, your tutor and/or practice assessor.

Comment

This activity provides a solid foundation for beginning the process of learning how to learn and reflecting on your preferred way of learning. This will be a continuing theme throughout this chapter. It is sometimes helpful to realise that you are not the only person who finds that learning can be both enhancing and difficult. It is useful to share our previous experiences of learning. It is also important for those who are employed to facilitate our learning, both academic and from practice, to be aware of what we find helpful to that process. Finally it is up to each of us to begin to take responsibility for our own learning and to try and deal with or avoid those experiences that block our learning.

CASE STUDY

In completing this activity Susan, a Year 1 student, realised that there had been a number of times during a lecture when she found it hard to listen, take notes and understand what she was hearing. She always had to go away and spend time reading over her notes and still felt she did not fully understand. On reflection she recognised that if she had prior access to the lecture notes she would learn better. So she approached the lecturer and asked if it was possible to have the lecture notes before the session. The lecturer agreed to post the lecture notes on the intranet a few days before each lecture. Susan then found with the opportunity to read ahead she was able to participate more fully in any discussion. Many of the other students were also grateful to Susan for making this request.

Reflective space

The idea of a reflective space is an important one for us. By this we mean both a physical space and the time to spend in it. A reflective space requires organisation and negotiation. Some of your social work courses will have negotiated this for you so far as your academic work is concerned. Study time will hopefully have been timetabled and space in university learning resource centres is there to be used. Of course some of your own time will be needed too. Ideally on placement a desk and regular supervision will form part of placement agreement meetings/contracts so that a reflective space is available there too, although this may not always be possible. It is important that the same negotiation and organisation occur in your domestic lives if you are to benefit from reflective activities. The level and amount of negotiation will vary according to your circumstances. If you are living in shared accommodation such as shared student houses, or living with partners and/or children, then it is very important to make your needs known and agreed. We recognise that a reflective space may sometimes be part of another activity such as having a bath or a shower, doing household tasks, waiting for a bus or a train. These sorts of spaces can be used productively and are often free of potential learning blocks that can be evoked by sitting at a desk. It helps us to realise how often we do in fact engage in reflection.

It is probably more challenging to secure a reflective space from work on post-qualifying social work courses but it is worth the effort to negotiate time and space from your line manager as it will be in your agency's interests that you enhance your learning and practice capabilities as a post qualified practitioner.

Experiential learning and the learning cycle

Most social work courses will use experiential learning techniques such as role play and simulation. So what are the components of learning by and from experience? Jenny Moon (1999, p20) says:

> that in general terms, the distinguishing features of experiential learning are that it refers to the organising and construction of learning from observations that have been made in some practical situation, with the implication that the learning can then lead on to action (or improved action).

Reflection is thus presumed to have a key role in experiential learning or in enabling experiential learning. On your qualifying social work course, over half of the course is spent in professional practice and probably quite a high proportion of university learning and teaching will also employ teaching methods which seek to value the experience you bring with you and create new/simulated experiences. Indeed the Department of Health provided a sum of money for each qualifying course to be used to provide skills laboratories to facilitate experiential learning. Generally such laboratories will have audiovisual equipment so that skills of good communication can be recorded and reflected upon. A good starting point is with an audio tape.

ACTIVITY 2.2

Using a tape recorder, begin by reading a short paragraph from a book. Once you have got the settings right, tape your response to the following questions and try to be as relaxed and conversational as possible.

- *What did I enjoy most on the course today?*
- *What learning stood out for me?*
- *What did I find uncomfortable or difficult?*

Comment

You may find that some important learning on the course does not happen in class but as a result of an informal interaction or incident that you were part of. Reflection on situations can help you to learn how you respond and also how you might wish you had responded. As you become more confident in using tapes you can then try taping a more conversational exchange with another student.

Models of learning

A major model of learning which you may encounter is the Kolb learning cycle.

Kolb's (1975) learning cycle includes the following concepts:

- concrete experience;
- observations and reflections;
- formation of abstract concepts and generalisations;
- testing implications of concepts in new situations.

Kolb makes the case that in order to be effective learners the four kinds of ability above are needed, which match the four stages of the learning cycle, namely, concrete experiencing of a situation, reflective observation, abstract conceptualisation and active experimentation. This whole idea of using reflection to turn experience into learning has been the subject of a number of books, not least that of Boud, Hough and Walker (1985). They see experiential learning operating both within the classroom as well as outside the classroom in professional practice. We would definitely concur with that conclusion. Boyd and Fales (1983), coming from an adult education and counselling perspective, see reflection as the key element in learning from experience in such a way that people are cognitively or affectively changed. The area of feeling and emotion is the focus of Chapter 3.

Learning styles

Following on from Kolb's learning cycle a number of self-evaluation questionnaires have been developed to help you explore what 'type' of learner you are. They tend to form part of study skills programmes and most social work courses will include this aspect of helping their students understand their preferences, styles and habits. Cottrell (2003) summarises and includes some of these questionnaires which students may like to access. At Chichester we have used one adapted from Kolb's work and also made reference to the work of Honey and Mumford (1982, 1992). Their terminology is similar to that of Kolb, as follows.

Activists prefer to work in an intuitive, flexible and spontaneous way, generating ideas and trying out new things. They usually have lots to say and contribute. They like to learn from experience, such as through problem-based learning, working in groups, workshops, discussion and teamwork

Reflectors prefer to watch and reflect, gathering data and taking time to consider all options and alternatives before making a decision. They prefer to learn through lectures, project work and working alone.

Theorists prefer to learn by going through things thoroughly and logically, step by step with clear guidelines, and have to feel they have learnt solidly before they apply what they know. They prefer to learn from books, problem-based learning and discussion.

Pragmatists prefer to learn by 'trying things out' to see if they work, just getting on with it, getting to the point. They like to be practical and realistic. They prefer to learn on work-based projects and practical applications.

ACTIVITY **2.3**

Look at the learning preferences as described above and decide which type best describes you and whether the associated way of learning matches your preferences.

Comment

You may have recognised that you have a preference for learning in a particular way and that may be a good starting point for you. You will need, however, to develop the other styles as most teachers will have a preference for teaching from a particular style, although good teachers will vary their methods so that all students can be engaged in the learning. Honey and Mumford (1982, 1992) offer a list of suggestions of exercises that will help you develop the full range of learning styles and thus become more competent learners.

CASE STUDY

Swaati, a very confident active student, always volunteered for role play and other experiential activities in class. However, she gradually realised that other students were learning more from the activity than she was. After completing a learning-style questionnaire she recognised that her reflector style needed some development. Consequently she began to pay more attention to recording thoughts and feelings and taking part in the post-activity discussion. She then began to make more sense of the theoretical material given out by the tutor and understand more of her learning from practice. In this way she had completed the learning cycle. She realised that she did not need to lead in role play and could learn by observing and listening to others.

What follows in this chapter are some of the activities that are used on the Chichester social work course, in the order that they are generally experienced. These activities may vary on other courses as we recognise that they can operate at different depths of learning.

Personal development planning (PDP)

All university students are being encouraged/required to undertake some form of PDP self-evaluation and Cottrell (2003) is very helpful in this respect. Many social work courses have used self-evaluation techniques for many years based on the premise that you need to know yourself before you try to know and work with other people in any deep or meaningful way. As stated above, Cottrell advocates starting early on reflection as part of a lifelong skill. She considers that the process of reflection has a number of elements as follows:

- making sense of the experience;
- standing back;
- repetition;
- deeper honesty;
- weighing up;
- clarity;
- understanding;
- making judgements.

Some of the activities in this chapter relate more closely to some of these elements than others.

Similarly, Thompson (2009) in the chapter on reflective practice in which he asserts that reflection is the essential process in applying theory to practice, lists the following activities as being essential to the promotion of reflective practice.

Reading Time spent reading is an investment and is not just for students but for all practitioners to give a broader perspective. After all, you are a social work student reading for a degree.

Asking First this applies to what you are reading so that you can make sense of what might be written in a jargonistic or academic style. It is also important to ask questions of tutors and each other and practitioners. Asking good questions is a vital skill for social workers. A social work assessment requires asking questions in a way that enhances engagement with people who use services and their carers and other professionals involved.

Watching There is much to be learned from an enhanced level of awareness in terms of observational skills and being sensitive to what is happening around us. Again this is explored in more detail below and in Chapter 3.

Feeling The emotional dimension of work with people must not be underestimated and thinking and feeling need to be synthesised in reflective practice. Chapter 3 explores this further.

Talking Sharing views and ideas about social work and social work practice encourages a broader perspective and a chance to learn from others' experiences. Constructive dialogue assists in broadening horizons, deepening understanding and enhancing skills.

Thinking A thoughtful approach to practice is essential if you are not to become routinised, which Thompson regards as a dangerous way of dealing with sensitive issues. Time pressures equally can militate against thinking carefully about actions (see Chapter 1).

Learning logs or journals

One of the most common ways of developing reflective practice used on social work courses is the use of learning logs or learning journals, so we will make this an early activity for getting started. Subsequent chapters also make reference to this important activity. We will use the term 'learning journal' although we appreciate that a variety of terminology may be used. The use of reflective journals is not restricted to professional courses and we recently heard of their use on such diverse undergraduate degrees as theology and media studies. The purposes of writing reflective journals are varied but may be, according to Moon (1999), to:

- record experience;
- develop learning in ways that enhances other learning;
- deepen the quality of learning;
- enable the learner to understand their own learning process;
- facilitate learning from experience;
- increase active involvement in learning;
- increase the ability to reflect and improve the quality of learning;
- enhance problem-solving skills;
- help assessment;
- enhance professional practice;
- explore the self, personal constructs and understand one's view of the world;
- enhance the valuing of the self towards self-empowerment;
- enable therapeutic purposes or as a means towards behaviour change;
- use as a means of slowing down learning, taking a more thorough account of a situation or situations;
- enhance creativity by making better use of intuitive understanding;

- free up writing and the representation of learning;

- provide an alternative voice for those not good at expressing themselves;

- foster reflective and creative interaction in a group.

You may have already discovered that some of your reflections might be difficult, possibly painful or upsetting. You may have tried to block or censor these reflections. As discussed in Chapter 1, it is important that this is shared either in supervision or tutorial. This will be explored further in the next chapter.

Guidance about the writing of journals may vary. On social work courses journals may be required to follow a particular structure or they may be totally unstructured. Our experience is that students prefer structured guidance in the early stages but can then develop their own style and structure. Essentially journals start off being rather descriptive but may quite quickly move to being more critically analytical about an event. Once the essential elements of a situation are described then this can be followed by some form of self-evaluation of personal experience, strengths, qualities and skills. Sometimes journals themselves are assessed or particular selections made from the journal are included in the form of a journal analysis. This means that you can remove those sections that are more private. They may, however, be shared in a tutorial or practice supervision.

At post-qualifying level the recording of one's social work career has been a part of portfolio building. The critical career review has been used on a number of post-qualifying programmes to demonstrate consolidation of competent social work practice.

Cottrell (2003) makes the important point that keeping a reflective journal can be very challenging, especially being motivated to making regular entries. It requires determination, good planning and a far-sighted approach. Being convinced of the value of the journal is paramount. It may be an overused process on some social work courses. Some useful exercises for getting started can include the following from Moon (1999), which draws quite heavily on the work of Progoff (1975).

- writing from different angles;

- metaphor;

- unsent letters;

- reflection on a book or reading assignment;

- using a critical friend;

- responding to set questions;

- describing the process of solving problems;

- focusing on a past experience;

- making lists;

- stepping stones from earliest memories;

- period reflections;

- imaginary dialogues with people;

- dialogues with events and projects;

- working with dreams and imagery.

It might be helpful to have a go at one or two of these to see if they help you to get started on journal writing. Alternatively try the next activity.

ACTIVITY 2.4

On your own:

Spend about 10–15 minutes composing a letter to a previous teacher or tutor, giving them positive feedback about how you experienced them in that role. Include your feelings and any outcomes of this experience, e.g. you inspired me to read Jane Austen, think about working with people, etc.

With another student:

Swap letters with your partner and take it in turns to role play being the recipient of the letter and meeting the writer to discuss it.

Comment

This activity builds on Activity 2.1 and enables you to be more concrete and specific about a previous learning experience and leads you to explore the consequences and implications for future learning. You could take this further by reflecting on the role play in your journal.

Blogging your reflection

You can use a blog to write reflectively about your learning experiences to provide a continuous record of your activities' progress and development. You may be familiar with travel blogs, often completed during 'gap' years where students write reflectively about their experience abroad. Where these are more than just a description of events, such as impressions and feelings, inviting comments from others, they can be part of the process of reflection.

A blog is an abbreviation of 'web log' and is designed as a web space that can be written to, published and viewed online. Blogs can be written about a wide variety of subjects and can also include audio (podcasting), video (vlog), photos (photoblog) as well as mobile blogs via a PDA (personal digital assistant).

The online blog is purely a tool which enables people to publish directly to a web space which is usually personal but it could also be set up as a group space if preferred. Typically, users register with a blog and then, as they log in, their passwords identify them to the blog. Users will be able to view their most recent entry to their blogs first and older entries are archived.

Blogs can be set up using commercially available spaces that use a hosting website, e.g. *www.blogger.com* or a restricted website where users have to be pre-registered, e.g. University Blog. Blogs can also be customised to meet the requirements of users, e.g. blog entries automatically trigger emails to supporting tutors to inform them that a new log entry has been published.

The advantage of writing reflectively online means that students can access their online logs or journals from any computer with internet access. If permissions are set up, students may choose to publish their reflective blogs to tutors, peers or to a worldwide audience.

Reflective blog entries can be structured to provide responses to set questions or left more open. Tutors or peers can provide formative feedback to blog entries that students can then respond to and set goals for their future learning. The blog can eventually form part or all of a summative assessment, providing evidence of learning achievements.

A micro-blog or tweet will allow you to send brief text updates or micro-media. These messages can be exchanged by a variety of means including texts, instant messaging email, digital audio or the web. The content of a micro-blog differs from traditional blogs in that it is smaller in actual size and aggregate file size, although its purpose is similar to the traditional blog. Probably the most well known is Twitter, founded in 2006, where entries are limited to 140 characters. Other leading social networking sites such as Facebook and MySpace also have their own micro-blogging features. All technical innovation has pros and cons and we are suggesting here that students use these to enhance their reflective practice.

ACTIVITY 2.5

Search the web and read some online blogs where people have reflected upon their learning. Look at how people reflect upon their learning and the style of language they use.

Register for your own online blog (e.g. www.blogger.com) or your university blog and post up your next learning reflections to your blog. If desired, email the web address to your tutor or peer and ask for some constructive feedback.

Comment

The activity should provide good insight into the variety of ways blogs can be presented and you should also recognise that the language used is often less formal than other forms of reflective writing. When writing a blog, remember that the last entry is always viewed first.

Peer feedback can be extremely beneficial and without involving the tutor, can be seen as less threatening by participants. Interestingly, peers who provide feedback can also learn through participation in the process to appreciate the value of creating constructive criticism, enabling students to become more critical and perceptive about their own learning (McConnell, 2006).

A final point about writing reflectively, particularly in journals and blogs, is that it is different to academic writing in the essential sense that it is written in the first person and not the third person. This may cause some students initial problems as they will have been encouraged in other writing to adhere to academic conventions. Rai (2006), writing about Open University students, noted that expectations for reflective journal writing seemed to contradict the usual academic conventions. She concludes that guidance for reflective writing such as reflective journals needs to be made explicit so that students are clear about the alternative conventions for reflective writing such as writing in the first person about the self, about feelings and about skill development, whether this is for learning and/or assessment.

Skills laboratory work

The Department of Health requires all social work courses to engage in some form of skills laboratory work and have provided each course with some funding to support this. Used sensitively and competently such laboratory work can greatly enhance student reflection on their performance, particularly in communication and interview skills. Students can undertake interview-type scenarios and are filmed doing so. These scenarios can either be previously prepared or they can arise from the student's own practice situations, such as might have been selected for presentation of a critical incident for analysis. Thus a more visual form of reflection is encouraged.

The resulting feedback acts as a mirror, as outlined in Chapter 1. You may find that having your skills recorded for analysis a frightening experience to begin with but eventually you will come to appreciate the learning that can be achieved by this form of reflection and analysis. Learning to give feedback to fellow students is a good skill to learn, as it is an important social work skill. The use of audio/visual recording methods helps to provide evidence to support the feedback. It also allows you to reflect on the skills you have demonstrated in the recording and be given guidance either from fellow students or tutors on how you can enhance your performance in future. The aim of all feedback is to encourage reflection on practice and provide ideas for improvement of performance.

ACTIVITY **2.6**

The importance of feedback in the reflective process cannot be underestimated so, in pairs:

- *Share with your partner some verbal or written feedback, that you have recently been given about your skills either from a skills laboratory workshop or from a practice assessor's observation of practice.*

- *Share how you responded to the feedback, e.g. were the comments unexpected, and whether you agreed or disagreed with them. What feelings were raised for you from the feedback?*

- *What steps you will take to improve your performance?*

- *Partner to give their response to what has been shared, including comment on any anti-oppressive issues.*

Repeat the exercise exchanging roles.

Comment

This exercise requires good listening skills, trust, respect and courage to share in a supportive space and to receive honest feedback. Try not to become complicit with your partner but to give praise where appropriate and also ideas for improvement, such as helpful resources including readings, web pages, people who might help, etc.

CASE STUDY

John was very anxious about being filmed in the skills laboratory and did all he could to avoid the experience. Eventually, however, he was encouraged to take part in a listening exercise in the laboratory. In spite of being nervous, the feedback he received from both students and staff was very encouraging. They told him that he appeared calm and confident, made good eye contact, his body language clearly showed that he was listening and his responses were thoughtful. He also learned that his voice was very quiet and he needed to develop his tone of voice and volume.

Non-verbal techniques

Much of what we have written in this chapter has been about verbal and written approaches to getting started in reflection. However, here are a number of non-verbal techniques that some students may find helpful. Others may find them less helpful. Some can be integrated with the verbal and written approaches.

Many students find these approaches to reflection both challenging and fun. They can be also used with service users for whom written and verbal approaches are difficult. Generally they come under what is termed 'right-brain activities' as follows:

- using aesthetic approaches such as drawing, sculpting, making collages, making or listening to music, composing a poem, etc.;
- graphical exercises such as drawing life lines or route maps;
- projective techniques such as photographs, pictures, film clips, audio clips;
- relaxation with guided fantasies;
- drama, including forum theatre techniques, role plays and simulations;
- concept mapping and organograms;
- using metaphor.

ACTIVITY 2.7

Draw, paint or make a collage from old magazines to show a metaphor for your own entry into social work. This can be done either with a partner or a small group.

Comment

Using different materials and approaches can release energy and encourage reflection in different ways. It can provide opportunity for fun and creativity and provide further insight into the process of reflection and the ways in which other students learn and develop.

Asking good questions

By making this a short separate section in this chapter we are emphasising the point that to be asked a good question either as a student or as a service user can be life enhancing and may promote deeper reflection. You will probably spend some time on your course developing good communication skills, and asking good questions is definitely worth the effort. Unfortunately in social work practice many questions are bureaucratically designed in the form of assessment forms and questionnaires. Nevertheless the ability to ask and be asked good questions enables deep reflection to take place. When we are asked a good question it seems to demand a thoughtful answer. Freud (1988, p110) says that asking good questions could have a liberating effect. She views good questions as gifts rather than intrusive assaults.

It is how a question is asked as well as what is asked that can make a good question. The more open a questions such as the 5WH formula is helpful. Who, What, When, Where, Why and How questions tend to suit thinkers who like to work in a logical, ordered or controlled way and appreciate some external direction. This is a good start but then it may be advisable to move on fairly quickly to open reflection, to go with the flow, let go, and be relatively unstructured, promoting free writing and thinking.

ACTIVITY **2.8**

What is the best question that you have been asked on your social work course? Why was it a good question? Have you asked the same question of other people? What was the response?

Comment

We hope that the answer to this activity is that you have been asked good questions and that they made you stop and think. According to Freud (1988), asking real questions means that you stand a chance of getting real answers, which may be upsetting, painful or disturbing and so you need to be able to bear the answers.

Critical incident analysis

The process of using critical incident analysis with social work students has been used for many years. Tutor groups meeting on a weekly or bi-weekly basis, during recall days from assessed practice placements, ask students to present to the group an analysis of an incident from their practice placement. The presentation includes:

- a brief description of the incident;

- an exploration of why the incident had a particular impact on you: what made it critical;

- an examination of which theoretical concepts informed your response and intervention;

- reflection on what has been learned from the incident and how it might inform future practice.

With the presentation, which is assessed, students submit a brief report of the incident. Following feedback on both the presentation and the report the student is then required to submit a longer evaluation of the critical incident, also for assessment, taking the learning from the incident further and placing it in a broader social context exploring issues of discrimination, inequality and oppression.

In 2005 the Scottish Institute for Excellence in Social Work Education (SIESWE) commissioned an evaluation of critical incident analysis as an innovative method of assessment (Crisp, BR, Green Lister, P and Dutton, K, 2004). The detailed report makes a case for critical incident analysis improving and enhancing social work students' learning, reinforcing our view that reflection on experiences in which the student is directly involved can lead to crucial learning without it being too onerous.

So what constitutes a critical incident? Our view is that it must be an incident that relates to an aspect of the student's own practice and it is their own actions in response to the incident that are reflected upon. It cannot be an incident in which they were an observer, however interesting that might be. This approach seems to concur with the SIESWE report. In it a critical incident is defined as one that causes us to think and reflect, that leads to learning about ourselves and others (individual and organisations) or about processes. Most incidents are not at all dramatic or obvious but commonplace events that occur routinely in social work education and/or professional practice. They may include any of the following situations:

- when you felt you had done something well;
- when you had made the wrong decision;
- when something went better than expected;
- when you lacked confidence;
- when you made a mistake;
- when you really enjoyed working with someone or a group;
- when you had a feeling of pressure;
- when you found it difficult to accept or value a service user(s);
- when you felt unsupported;
- when you were worried about a service user(s);
- when you took a risk and it paid/didn't pay off.

Crisp, BR, Green Lister, P, and Dutton K. (2004) devised a five-stage framework for the analysis, which generally covers the same areas that Chichester students are asked to follow, apart from the exploration of the theoretical base, as follows:

- account of the incident;

- initial response to the incident;

- issues and dilemmas highlighted by the incident;

- outcomes;

- learning.

ACTIVITY 2.9

Select an incident from your practice and use the framework above to reflect on and analyse the incident. This is a useful exercise to complete in pairs in the first instance.

Comment

What sort of incident did you select for analysis? Was it dramatic or commonplace? It is important that you are aware that the term 'critical' does not necessarily mean dramatic or negative.

It is very likely that you will be asked to undertake something similar on your course, with the analysis of the critical incident being used for either formative or summative assessment. For most of our students completing these in groups it is an important element of learning from reflection (reflection-on-action) from our own and others' experiences. We agree with Thompson that thinking about theory and how it has informed the practice is an important element in critical incident analysis.

Narrative analysis

As suggested in Chapter 1, social work practice is often complex and messy and reflections on practice frequently reflect this. It is important therefore to try to reflect on your reflections and this we are calling narrative analysis. This is probably a section of the chapter that may be more relevant for post-qualifying students, especially those who are training to become practice assessors and/or mentors.

Many of us find meaning in our lives from the stories or narratives that we ourselves tell or hear about ourselves, our families and friends, etc. 'Story' is taken to mean the actual events while 'narrative' is the recounting of the story. Taylor (2006, p193) says that we grasp our lives in narrative – it enables us to make sense, to pattern the events of our lives. She adopts a dialogical approach to narrative, involving a narrator and an audience, attending to the interactive/performance aspects of narrative rather than its formal properties. She goes on to make the important point that in social work education reflective accounts in the form of journals, diaries, etc., tend to be taken as 'what really happened' in any situation whereas it should be recognised that narrators select, order and report events in particular ways for particular effects. This may be particularly the case when reflective accounts or commentaries are being assessed. Students will try to structure their journals to meet the requirements for a pass grade and try and write what they think the assessor wants to read. In Taylor's analysis they are performing two closely connected identities, one as the competent and caring professional and the other as competent reflector, forming a composite identity as the 'reflective practitioner' (Taylor, 2006, p195). Of course this is what this book is attempting to promote and so are social work courses that value the reflective approach. It needs to be authentic and genuine and not 'just for the sake of'.

The aim of a narrative is to persuade the listener or reader that the story is true and that the author is to be believed. It is important that in telling the story we trust what the narrator is telling us. Both the narrator and the story need to ring true. Sometimes what helps in narration is the inclusion of actual dialogue, as this aids authenticity. In persuading the listener/reader of the veracity of the story, the inclusion of reflections on practice will help so that the narrative is not just a descriptive account but something that promotes deeper learning about the professional identity of the social worker and their view of the world of the service user. Students writing narratives and staff responsible for their assessment need to bear this in mind as they undertake their respective difficult and responsible tasks. A case could be made that such narratives should not be used for assessment but rather for formative development. We consider that assessment is part of learning and that sensitive assessment, carefully carried out and moderated, is worth the time and effort.

ACTIVITY **2.10**

Reflect back on all the activities that we have asked you to do in this chapter and in pairs identify themes/patterns that have emerged from your narratives and share them with your partner. Alternatively, if you are in placement or post-qualifying, reflect on a story that you have been told by a service user or carer for its authenticity and veracity.

Comment

This kind of reflection draws upon many of the skills already mentioned in this chapter such as observation and critical incident analysis. It is a profound part of your development as a professional.

C   H   A   P   T   E   R   S   U   M   M   A   R   Y

In this chapter we have introduced you to a number of ways of getting started in reflecting on your practice and learning how to learn. All the activities are practical and each one builds on the previous activities, helping you to develop your reflective skills. We have illustrated how adults learn and why reflective practice is worth the effort. We have also discussed a wide range of ways in which your reflections will be central to your learning and practice as a social worker. Some of the ideas we have presented will appeal more than others and this of itself is worthy of reflection. We hope that you will enjoy getting started and have learned more about yourself as a reflective practitioner. It is important to know what works for you and what you need to develop.

*FURTHER
READING*

The following three books provide a good general overview of the practical skills of reflection, theory and its application to social work practice.

Cottrell, S (2003) *Skills for success: The personal development planning guide*. Basingstoke: Palgrave Macmillan.

Thompson, N (2009) *People skills*. 3rd edition. Basingstoke: Palgrave Macmillan.

Moon, JA (2004) *A handbook of reflective and experiential learning: Theory and practice*. London: RoutledgeFalmer.

Part Two
Developing the reflective practitioner

Chapter 3
Reflecting on emotion in social work

Gill Butler

There are no references to understanding or working with feelings and emotions in the National Occupational Standards (NOS), Subject Benchmark statement or General Social Care Council Code of Conduct. However, in my view and that of the authors whose work I will draw on, the ability to understand our own and others' emotions is central to effective social work practice. To ignore this aspect of human relationships in social work is rather like trying to discuss the physical nature of the world with someone who is only aware of two dimensions of existence and thinks that the world is flat, rather than a three-dimensional sphere.

A C H I E V I N G   A   S O C I A L   W O R K   D E G R E E

By enhancing your awareness of the third dimension of practice, this chapter will be especially helpful in enabling you to meet the following National Occupational Standards.
Key Role 2: Plan, carry out, review and evaluate social work practice, with individuals, families, carers, groups, communities and other professionals
Key Role 4: Manage risk to individuals, families, carers, groups, communities, self and colleagues
Key Role 6: Demonstrate professional competence in social work practice

It will also introduce you to the following academic requirements as set out in the Quality Assurance Agency (QAA) social work subject benchmark statement (2000).
2.2.4 Defining principles
Social workers should be equipped both to understand, and to work within, this context of contested debate about nature, scope and purpose.
• Enabled to analyse, adapt to, manage and eventually to lead the processes of change.
• Practise in ways that maximise safety and effectiveness in situations of uncertainty and incomplete information.
3.1.5 The nature of social work practice
The nature and characteristics of skills associated with effective practice, both direct and indirect, with a range of service users and in a variety of settings, including group-care.
3.2.2.4 Intervention and evaluation
• Build and sustain purposeful relationships with people and organisations in community-based and inter-professional contexts including group-care.
• Manage the complex dynamics of dependency and, in some settings, provide direct care and personal support in everyday living situations.
3.2.4 Skills in working with others
• Develop effective helping relationships with other individuals, groups and organisations that facilitate change.

> **3.2.5 Skills in personal and professional development**
> - Advance their own learning and understanding with a degree of independence.
> - Reflect on and modify their behaviour in the light of experience.
> - Identify and keep under review their own personal and professional boundaries.
> - Manage uncertainty, change and stress in work situations.
> - Handle inter-personal and intra-personal conflict constructively.
> - Understand and manage changing situations and respond in a flexible manner.
> - Challenge unacceptable practices in a responsible manner.
> - Take responsibility for their own further and continuing acquisition of knowledge and skills.

Television…thrives on unreason (and)… strikes at the emotions rather than the intellect.

(Robin Day, *Grand Inquisitor*, 1989)

The problem is … how to remain whole in the midst of the distractions of life; how to remain balanced, no matter what centrifugal forces tend to pull one off centre; how to remain strong, no matter what shocks come in at the periphery and tend to crack the hub of the wheel.

(Morrow Lindbergh, 2002)

Introduction

The quotations above raise two of the critical issues that this chapter will help you to consider. The first typifies comments that juxtapose emotion and reason. Society and the organisations that we work in are informed by this way of thinking, and we need to consider what impact this has on social work practice. The second quotation reflects the dilemma for many busy social work practitioners, feeling pulled in all directions by competing needs which can be emotionally draining. This chapter will endeavour to provide you with a greater awareness of what is happening in such situations and some strategies for staying 'whole'.

As I have suggested above, understanding feelings and emotions is essential, if we are to understand the complicated, often messy, emotionally charged situations which social workers are faced with. The ability to deal with such situations well will be extremely helpful for those you work with, colleagues, service users and carers, as well as deeply rewarding for you. Developing a language to express and explore emotions is therefore crucial. We will begin this chapter by exploring some of the difficulties associated with the current use of language, which is heavily influenced by managerialism. This cloaks the reality of social work practice in which the need to be able to understand and process our own and others' emotions is central to many of the interactions that take place. Careful reflection can provide the vehicle for doing this. As we will see, the absence of such understanding can be associated with notable failures in social work, where the workers have been unaware of what I have called the third dimension, so have been unable to recognise what is happening.

By the end of this chapter you will have an increased awareness of the:

- significance of language;

- nature of emotion;

- impact of emotion on social work practice;

- role of reflection in understanding and managing our own and others' emotional responses.

The problem with feelings and emotion

Hugman (2005) argues that reason has dominated the development of Western philosophical thinking as the basis for determining what is good. This creates difficulties, which are compounded by thinking in a way that is described as dualistic (Bock and James, 1992). By that we mean that we think in terms of either/or, e.g. black or white, male or female, good or bad. We also tend to think in terms of one state being preferable to the other; this is known as asymmetric dualism. The positive qualities of one imply that the other is negative, or less desirable. This way of thinking can unconsciously limit our ability to appreciate difference. As a result, rather than seeing emotion as different from reason, it is defined in opposition to reason as unreliable and subjective (Hugman, 2005, p48). Often we feel embarrassed by talking about our feelings, or worry that we may be seen as irrational. This might be the case, but it is also possible that emotion is informing what we say and do appropriately. Gender issues also need to be considered, as traditionally working with emotions is an area of work that has been largely invisible, undertaken primarily by women and conflated with notions of women's 'natural' caring role (Smethurst, 2004). It is perhaps not surprising that in a profession where the importance of technical and managerial skills are emphasised, rational, analytical thinking is prioritised. In reality emotion and reason are not opposite sides of a coin, but are intimately connected.

The significance of language in the construction of social work practice

Until recently relatively little attention has been paid to the significance of language as both reflecting and shaping notions of effective social work practice (Gregory and Holloway, 2005). However, by writing and talking practitioners and academics demonstrate what they are preoccupied with and believe to be important. The language used in legislation and policy has the power to shape practice in a top-down way, whereas the user and carer movements have exerted power from the bottom up by challenging the labels applied to them by professionals. This is discussed further in Chapter 5. The changing nature of social work is thus revealed through the language that is used.

A historical perspective

Gregory and Holloway (2005) outline stages in the development of social work. They describe the initial phase as a moral enterprise. Its roots came from the work of the social reformers at the end of the nineteenth century, who endeavoured to reform the morals of those who, as a result of their moral weakness, lived in impoverished circumstances. A good example of the language which reflects their concerns can be found in this list from the NSPCC in 1901, which identifies the following child abusing types:

The devil–may-care and idler;
The drunkard;
The married and unfaithful;
The married and estranged;
The unmarried;
The tramp;
The better and gambler;
The speculator in child life insurance;
The avaricious and greedy.

This reformist approach broadly persisted until the 1950s when therapeutic psycho-social approaches gained in popularity. Here the aim was to treat people, who were defined as clients, with a focus on the individual and interpersonal relationships. The work of Biestek (1961) was highly influential. He identified seven principles which he considered essential to effective practice. Of these the first two focus directly on the emotional component of practice and the other five also pay attention to the nature of the 'client/worker' relationship:

purposeful expression of feelings;
controlled emotional involvement;
individualisation;
acceptance;
non-judgemental attitude;
client self-determination;
confidentiality.

In the 1970s the Marxist analysis presented by radical social workers endeavoured to challenge the individualistic focus of therapeutic social work, locating problems within the context of structural inequality. The aims of radical social workers described by Bailey and Brake (1975) were:

education (development of critical consciousness);
systems linking;
counter-systems building.

However, alongside this, treatment-based problem-solving approaches continued to form the basis for mainstream social work practice.

In the 1980s the language used began to shift again to focus on the tasks that were expected of social workers. Confidence in social work was at a low ebb, which opened the door for increasing bureaucratisation and the steady rise of managerialism. Language from this period on reflects the emphasis on following procedures, achieving outcomes, evidence-based practice and key performance indicators as a way to address perceived failures in practice. There is an emphasis on technical proficiency and empirical data as the essential platform for competent performance of the tasks required of social workers. The limitations of this approach are demonstrated in the National Occupational Standards for social work (NOS). Ostensibly they provide a framework for developing the competence required of a 'beginning social worker' and provide a model representing the holistic nature of social work practice. However, by framing this entirely in terms of values, roles and tasks, the affective or third dimension of practice is invisible. There are no references to feelings, emotions or indeed reflection, but 17 references to managing. There is a similar absence of references to emotion and feeling in the subject benchmark statement.

In a climate where the defensive adherence to procedures is seen as a vital mechanism to ensure survival and avoid the possibility of blame or criticism, it is arguably difficult for social work to maintain a focus on the significance of relationships and feelings. Technical rationality may also be more attractive to an emerging profession seeking to gain status alongside established professional groups. However, knowledge, skills and rational thought may not be sufficient to equip us to respond effectively when faced with a range of powerful emotions, such as grief, fear, anger and hostility, which, as will be discussed later, are central to social work practice.

The impact of emotion on social work practice

RESEARCH SUMMARY

There have been several important critiques of the Laming report (2003) into the death of Victoria Climbié in 2000 (Ferguson, 2005; Foster, 2005; Rustin, 2005). While the focus is primarily on issues raised in relation to child protection, they also have wider relevance to social work practice. The inquiry carefully details the many missed opportunities to recognise the tragic circumstances of Victoria's life and highlights the failure to do 'the simple things properly'. Resource issues, poor inter-professional communication, inexperience, failures in accountability and poor management are seen as the major reasons for the failure to protect Victoria. However, the inquiry fails to move from the relatively superficial, albeit meticulous presentation of the data, to an in-depth exploration of why on this, as well as on notable previous occasions, despite working very hard, practitioners were unable to attribute meaning to what they were seeing and to recognise the deep distress of the child. This was illustrated by the comment of one social worker who had said that Victoria looked like an advert for Action Aid.

It is argued that this state of *seeing but not seeing, knowing and not knowing* needs to be understood from a psychoanalytic perspective. We can then begin to understand that the difficulties may be seen as defence mechanisms operating to protect the workers. If we deny what we see and what we feel, then we do not have to acknowledge the true horror of the situation, which feels unbearable. It therefore removes the need for workers to take action to protect Victoria, so protecting them from a potentially very frightening experience, given the power of her aunt (Ferguson, 2005). Cooper and Lousada (2005) explore the pervasiveness of these defensive mechanisms in relation to the wider development of social policy and organisational practice.

The summary above provides a helpful illustration of the difficulty for practitioners faced with deeply distressing and frightening situations, which may result in the worker being unable to act, because the feelings aroused are unbearable and therefore denied. They may also be denied because we are not confident about the valuable role of feelings as an invaluable source of information, for some of the reasons outlined above. We may dismiss our fears and anxieties as irrational feelings, to be kept private.

Difficulties may also arise in relation to very different situations as in the case study below, where feelings of loss are evoked and avoided.

CASE STUDY

Vivienne is a student who came to Britain from Zimbabwe five years ago. She has tape-recorded an interview in preparation for an assignment where she will be required to analyse her communication skills. The tape recording is played back in the tutorial group, which provides Vivienne with an opportunity to receive feedback from the group.

The interviewee was seeking asylum. When she started to speak about her sadness in relation to home and members of her family who were left behind, the student interviewer responded by asking her about her financial difficulties and benefits. When asked by her tutor why she had done this, her initial response was that she had changed the subject because she did not want to upset the interviewee.

ACTIVITY 3.1

Write down a list of feelings that the interviewee was conveying to the interviewer.

How might the interviewer have felt as she listened to this?

Why?

What effect might changing the subject have had on the interviewee?

Comment

In the previous section we have considered some examples that demonstrate the difficulties that can arise when practitioners are unable or unwilling to recognise the feelings of others. As we have seen, we may do this in some situations to protect ourselves from those feelings and to remove the need to respond to the situation. In other situations that are less threatening, we may still lack confidence and so fail to pay sufficient attention to the emotional dimension of the interaction. As a result our responses are not attuned to the needs of the service user and may be experienced as unhelpful or inappropriate, as in the example of Vivienne.

The absence of a language to identify the significance of the emotional component of practice exacerbates the problem. If as suggested earlier, emotion is contrasted with reason we may not recognise the value of exploring the emotional component of practice, paying close attention to the affective elements of communication and systematically analysing feelings.

In the next sections we will attempt to address these difficulties by exploring the language of feelings and emotions in more depth and considering their role. We will then draw on the work of Solway developed by Goleman (1996) and constructs from psychoanalytic theory to help us to understand and work with feelings and emotions more effectively.

Defining emotion

Emotions are strong feelings arising from an altered state of mind. They engage all aspects of the brain and therefore have the power to disrupt thought (McLannahan, 2004). They may be accompanied by physiological responses. They may arise rapidly in response to certain stimuli, so if we reflect we are usually able to identify the trigger. Emotions are usually conscious and have an object, e.g. a person who has made you angry. They are also therefore part of the process of making judgements (he has made you angry because you are upset by his treatment of his partner) and so reveal our values. It is usually possible to identify a trigger for the emotion, which may only last a short time in the absence of the trigger (when he leaves the room your anger subsides). Whilst there is some debate about how many basic emotions there are, most would include happiness, sadness, anger, fear, surprise, anticipation and disgust. Other emotions such as envy, shame and gratitude may be seen as stemming from or arising from various combinations of these.

Moods do not usually have an object, are less intense, longer-lasting affective states that may affect the way we view things. Often we may be unclear about what has caused the mood. As they are more muted than emotions they may have a less immediate impact on our responses.

ACTIVITY 3.2

This activity would be best completed with a partner.

1 *Write down a list of as many words to describe feelings that you can think of.*
   Underline the feeling words that you use regularly.
   Share this list with your partner. Notice similarities and differences. Explore possible reasons for this (e.g. culture, gender, age).

2 *Make another list of the emotions that you have felt in the last two days.*
   * *Try to identify the triggers that caused you to feel these emotions.*
   * *Identify what you were doing at the time when you felt each emotion.*
   * *Consider the strength of the emotional responses that you have listed. Were they mild, moderate or intense?*

Comment

Whilst there are hundreds of words that we can use to discuss emotion, in practice our vocabularies tend to be restricted. Our fluency in identifying, expressing and evaluating feelings will have an impact on our ability to process them and will enhance our ability to support others in expressing their feelings.

The role of emotion

Emotions can serve an important purpose in alerting us to the potential need to alter our goals. Originally this may have been to ensure survival, hence the importance of very rapid emotional responses (McLennahan, 2004). Sometimes we call these responses gut feelings or instinct. It is important to recognise their function and pay attention to them. Goleman draws a distinction between the rational and the feeling mind and suggests that there needs to be a balance between them if we are to think clearly and make wise decisions. The emotional mind is associative, so may react to the present as though it were the past (Goleman, 1998).

Emotion is closely linked to motivation, so what we feel will influence our actions. You may know that you need to have written 1000 words by the end of the day in order to have your essay completed on time, but if you feel upset by something you may be unable to motivate yourself to do this, although rationally you know that you should. A good understanding of the relationship between emotion, cognition and actions will enable us to harness our emotions in order to act more appropriately and achieve our goals.

CASE STUDY

It is Friday afternoon and I am planning to make sure my case records are up to date, as I will not be in until Wednesday next week.

I have been working with a woman who is thought to have some degree of learning difficulty. She is pregnant and is the mother of two small children. They were referred to social services by the health visitor, who has concerns about her ability to cope with a third child and about the developmental progress of the children. She says the mother avoids contact and is dismissive. The case is seen as low priority (Children Act 1989 section 17) and appropriate for a student.

Over the last fortnight during the course of two visits she tells me that her partner does not think this third baby is his. On the second occasion she was tearful and mentions that her partner came home the other night rather the worse for wear. She hesitates then assures me he is very good with his kids and that she can cope without any help. The children are appropriately dressed and have some toys. They are very quiet and seem undemanding and rather subdued.

ACTIVITY 3.3

Working in pairs, identify a situation where you have not done what you think you should have done.

Take a sheet of paper and write three headings: Intended action, What I actually did, Feelings at the time. Complete the columns with reference to the situation that you have identified. An example of what this might look like in relation to the situation that I have just described is provided in Figure 3.1.

ACTIVITY 3.3 *continued*

Intended action	What I actually did	Feelings at the time
Write up case notes from the visits in order to discuss them with my manager next week.	Had a cup of tea, chatted to a colleague about plans for the weekend. Made some phone calls to set up some non-urgent visits.	Unsettled Rather low Worried, but not sure about what

Figure 3.1

Discuss with your partner:

The relationship between your thoughts about what you plan to do, your feelings and your actions.

Consider how it might help/hinder you if you are more aware of the relationship between your thoughts, actions and feelings.

Emotion and critical thinking

There is increasing recognition of the role of emotion in critical thinking and deep learning. Moon (2005) identifies an approach that *includes emotional as well as cognitive and whole person functioning*. Clearly the ability to think critically is essential for social workers, but the importance of emotion in this process is not always recognised. Sometimes there is a mistaken belief that we must just concentrate on the facts.

RESEARCH SUMMARY

Ruch (2005) found in her research that it was possible to categorise reflective practitioners into two broad groupings of technical or holistically orientated practitioners. She found that the former tended to concentrate on practical issues and were principally concerned with reviewing what had happened and how it had happened in order to improve their practice. The holistic practitioners included these aspects of reflection, but in addition considered why things had or had not happened. She found that the holistic practitioners paid greater attention to emotional processes and were more aware of the importance of self-awareness. This facilitated responsive, relationship based approaches to practice. As a result they were also more able to tolerate uncertainty and risk.

Developing emotional intelligence

The concept of emotional intelligence is based on a recognition of the crucial role of emotion in influencing cognitive thought and determining what we do. The emotionally intelligent person is thus able to sense, understand and use emotions in order to improve their own effectiveness and their relationships with others (**www.6seconds.org**). Whilst there are mixed views about the value of some of the work on emotional intelligence and the claims made in relation to its success in improving effectiveness, it can provide a helpful framework for developing emotional literacy. This involves being able to recognise what you are feeling so that it informs your understanding and enables you to act appropriately. Such a definition suggests that emotional literacy could be key in helping practitioners in the emotional minefields of practice, where the ability to be able to accurately identify our own feelings and those of others in order to be able to act appropriately is crucial, as identified in the case of Victoria Climbié.

Self-awareness

Goleman's (1998) work on emotional intelligence recognises emotional self-awareness as an essential first stage of using emotion effectively. He draws a distinction between characteristics of emotional competence in relation to self which is referred to as personal competence and in relation to interactions with others, social competence. The model then moves on to provide a framework which suggests that as we develop greater awareness, we can begin to regulate our behaviour in order to be more effective, both personally and socially, as summarised in Figure 3.2.

	Self: Personal competence	Other: Social competence
1. Awareness	Self-awareness Emotional self-awareness Accurate self-assessment Self-confidence	Social awareness Empathy Service orientation Organisational awareness
2. Regulation / Action	Self-control Ability to soothe ourselves Ability to delay gratification Conscientiousness Adaptability Achievement Drive Initiative	Attuned responses Effective communication Ability to manage conflict Provide leadership Change catalyst Collaborative

Figure 3.2

(Adapted from *www.eiconsortium.org* with permission)

The reflective activities suggested earlier in this chapter are designed to help with the first stage of emotionally competent practice, by developing your ability to notice and then to accurately identify an expanded range of emotions. Through conscious reflection we can develop our awareness of our feelings and what has triggered them. We can then start to focus on the feelings of others, noticing and reflecting on their meaning. One way of doing this is by exploring our responses to particular triggers in small groups. Visual stimuli such as photographs or excerpts from television programmes, documentaries and films can be used for this purpose as they encourage emotionally direct writing.

ACTIVITY 3.4

With a partner, or in small groups:

Watch a 5–10 minute extract from a film or television programme (programmes such as Super Nanny provide useful material). Do not take any notes, just observe. Afterwards write down:

- *What you saw. Do this as a free-flowing narrative.*
- *What you felt when you were watching it.*
- *The feelings, as you perceived them, of the actors.*
- *Your feelings now as you write this up. Include any other memories, thoughts or feelings that were stirred by this process and record them.*

Share your responses with your partner and discuss the similarities and differences in your observations and the feelings that this experience evoked.

Comment

This activity will help you to be more aware of your own emotional responses. It will also demonstrate how subjective your observations are. No two people will feel or see exactly the same things in any situation. Often there are different opinions and feelings about the same event. This exercise may help you to be more open-minded and less judgemental about how each of us perceives the world. Observations are influenced by previous experience as well as differences such as gender, age, disability, race, sexuality and other diversities.

Child observation

Some social work courses include the opportunity to undertake a series of observations of an infant or young child, using an adaptation of a method originally developed for training child psychoanalysts and pioneered at the Tavistock Clinic. Students are asked to write up their observations in a similar way to that suggested above and then to present them to a small seminar group. This can be a helpful way of developing our self awareness, particularly in relation to understanding where feelings may be coming from, as memories of our own previous experiences of being parented and/or parenting are often stirred by this process. Trowell and Miles (1996) suggest that:

> social workers need to be capable of taking an observational stance to give themselves the possibility of objectivity in coming to their conclusions. The observational stance requires them to be aware of the environment, the verbal and non-verbal interaction; to be aware of their own responses as a source of invaluable data, provided that they are aware of what comes from them and what comes from their clients; and to develop the capacity to integrate these and give themselves time to think before arriving at a judgement or making a decision. (p125)

The ability to use our responses as a source of information may enrich our practice greatly and enable us to understand the meaning of some of the difficult and painful situations that we may be faced with. However, the need to be aware of what comes from us, and what comes from others, is critical. Good supervision is clearly essential, as is an understanding of the processes of transference and counter transference.

Transference

Sometimes when we say something to someone we are taken aback by their response, which seems to us to have been out of all proportion or unrelated to what we have said. If we are surprised in this way, it is useful to consider whether transference may have taken place.

The concept of transference was first identified by Freud, who noticed that not only were his patients' reactions sometimes unrelated to anything that was taking place in his relationship with him, but also they had fantasies about him that bore no relation to reality (Conner, 2001). From this he developed a theory that their responses might be triggered by a memory of an earlier experience, which unconsciously then determined their feelings and responses in the present relationship with him. This phenomenon is consistent with the research noted by Goleman (1998), leading to his conclusion that the emotional mind may react to the present as though it were the past. Transference reactions may be positive or negative. I may for example assume that someone who enjoys a particular food that reminds me of my father, of whom I have fond memories, is a kind and patient person, when in fact there is no evidence to support this assumption. Similarly, I may find myself wondering why I am finding it hard to work with someone, who reminds me of someone I knew and disliked as a teenager, and happens to have the same name. Examples of transference are often found in the educational context.

CASE STUDY

Linda is a student plagued by fear of failure and unable to talk about this, either to her tutor, who she knows has been very supportive to other students, or in the tutor group that she has been part of for two years. This is a supportive group and other students in it often gain support from each other by sharing problems and exchanging ideas. She has obtained good results on the course so far, but believes that somehow this must just be luck, which is bound to change soon. Linda is convinced that the other members of her tutor group will make fun of her if she discusses her anxieties and that she will be exposed as being stupid. As a child she was bullied, failed her eleven-plus and did poorly in her GCSE examinations. Her school teachers seemed disinterested in her.

Counter-transference

This is a related concept, where your own (repressed) feelings are unconsciously placed on the other person. If we continue with the example of Linda, her tutor starts to wonder if she has the ability to help her, and wonders if Linda will ever make any progress.

ACTIVITY 3.5

Identify an interaction on placement where you are left thinking, 'Why did they react like that?' How can you use your understanding of transference to further your understanding of interactions with service users and colleagues?

Regulation and action: emotionally intelligent practice

The reflective activities so far have helped us to notice what is happening in relation to our own feelings and those of others, so that we are more personally and socially aware, congruent and empathic. We can then move on to focus on considering how we can utilise this awareness to regulate or channel our energy and act in such a way that we have harnessed the insight that we have gained. This can help us to behave in ways that are socially skilled and assist in managing emotion in our relationships with others. Again, reflection can provide a pathway to achieving this. In the next case study the social worker uses reflection to ensure that he communicates effectively and works in a collaborative rather than a confrontational way.

CASE STUDY

Dave, a social worker in a busy community learning disability team, is checking his emails. He has five minutes before he needs to leave to go to a case conference involving a service user whom he has been working with. He is anticipating that it will be difficult as the child care team are extremely critical of her parenting. Dave feels they have failed to provide adequate support and are patronising towards her. He opens an email from the manager of a local day centre, headed URGENT. The email is personally critical and demands an immediate response from Dave as he has not completed all the details on a referral form that he recently sent through. The email further states that they will not deal with the referral until he has done so. Dave knew it would be difficult to find these details and considered that the referral needed urgent action. He notices that it has been copied to his manager. He is tempted to reply angrily, but instead, prints out the email, in order to reflect before he responds. Later Dave reads the email again and writes down:

- *what was happening when he received the email;*
- *how he felt when he received the email;*
- *what he thought the manager might have been feeling when she sent the email;*
- *what he feels now;*
- *how he might channel his feelings to use them constructively;*
- *what actions might be helpful to ensure that his long-term goals are achieved.*

(continued)

CASE STUDY *continued*

He was then able to respond appropriately to the email, recognising that they were both under pressure; his need was to ensure that a service was provided, but she needed the additional information in order to deliver an appropriate service.

It can also be helpful when reflecting to consider the impact of your feelings on your:

- *communication with others;*
- *energy levels;*
- *ability to complete routine tasks;*
- *ability to make decisions.*

Comment

The impact of emotion on the achievement of goals can be very positive, so it is useful to reflect on both positive and apparently negative experiences. The particular value of writing about difficult experiences and our feelings about them has been highlighted in research by Pennebaker (2007). He found that people who had been made redundant who were required to write about this on four consecutive days for 15 minutes a day were more likely to succeed in finding another job, as they were able to process their anger, achieve insight and channel their actions to achieve their new goals. In a similar study improvements were found in people's physical well-being, as measured through their immune systems (Pennebaker, 1997).

C H A P T E R   S U M M A R Y

Language both reflects and shapes social work practice, so it is important that we pay attention to the language used in policy and the language that you use in practice. Emotion has been marginalised, often seen as hindering rational thought, when in reality reason and emotion are complementary rather than opposing states of awareness, so recognition of emotion is needed if you are to understand the meaning of a situation. Failure to recognise this dimension of practice will at the least be seen to miss the point and at worst may result in an inability to recognise tragic situations. It is therefore essential that your reflection includes this third dimension of reflection on emotion. The importance of good supervision in supporting this process will be discussed further in Chapter 9.

The development of emotional intelligence through reflection on emotion may hold the key to enabling you to remain a whole person who can practise holistically. The reflective exercises outlined above and in the first chapter will help you with this.

Cooper, A and Lousada, J (2005) *Borderline welfare: Feeling and fear of feeling in modern welfare.* London: Karnac.
Coming from a psychodynamic perspective the authors explore in much greater depth the significance of defence mechanisms that operate to protect society from certain forms of feeling. The impact of this on policy and practice is explored and includes an excellent analysis of the Laming report.

Goleman, D (2004) *Emotional intelligence and working with emotional intelligence.* London: Bloomsbury.
A good introduction to emotional intelligence for those who would like to explore this further.

www.eiconsortium.org

Useful website with examples of research into a range of approaches to developing emotional intelligence.

Chapter 4

Reflection as a catalyst for change

Gill Constable

ACHIEVING A SOCIAL WORK DEGREE

This chapter will begin to help you meet the following National Occupational Standards.

Key Role 1: Prepare for, and work with individuals, families, carers, groups and communities to assess their needs and circumstances

- Prepare for social work contact and involvement.
- Work with individuals, families, carers, groups and communities to help them make informed decisions.
- Assess needs and options to recommend a course of action.

Key Role 2: Plan, carry out, review and evaluate social work practice, with individuals, families, carers, groups, communities and other professionals

- Interact with individuals, families, carers, groups and communities to achieve change and development and to improve life opportunities.

Key Role 5: Manage and be accountable, with supervision and support, for your own social work practice within your organisation

- Manage and be accountable for your own work.

The following social work subject benchmark statements relate to this chapter.

Managing problem-solving activities

- Think logically and systematically
- Plan a sequence of actions to achieve specified objectives
- Manage the processes of change

Skills in personal and professional development

- Reflect on and modify their behaviour in the light of experience
- Manage uncertainty, change and stress in work situations.

Introduction

This chapter will focus on the use of reflection to develop personal and professional effectiveness. The process of reflection will be underpinned by the development of critical thinking skills in addition to techniques derived from cognitive and behavioural theories; in particular, Ellis's (1999) ABC theory found within rational emotive behaviour therapy.

Social work is a profession with reported higher levels of stress-related ill health such as musculoskeletal disorders, depression and anxiety, than other occupational groups (Health and Safety Executive, 2004). It is important then that we do not neglect the opportunity to develop our emotional resilience, as this will impact on our attitude and behaviour towards service users and carers, as well as the quality of our life. These approaches can be shared with users and carers to help them manage stressful and difficult experiences.

The chapter will begin by giving some definitions and explanations of what is meant by reflection. An exploration will then take place of what cognitive and behavioural theories are, and how they can be applied with particular reference to patterns of thinking and behaviour that are disempowering. A number of approaches will be discussed, such as:

- defining critical thinking skills;
- writing reflectively;
- self-talk and belief systems;
- developing self-acceptance.

The chapter will follow Suzy, a student social worker, on her assessed practice placement. Suzy developed her capacity to reflect, which helped her to manage herself when working with complex and stressful situations. Suzy's progress through her placement will be structured around the ASPIRE model of assessment (Sutton, cited by Parker and Bradley, 2003).

Throughout the chapter there will be several exercises for you to do that will enable you to understand how the theory and the methods arising from it can be put into use.

What do we understand by reflection?

A definition of reflection in terms of social work practice was discussed in Chapter 1. If we now return to this, Horner (2004) suggests that reflection is a prerequisite to being an effective social worker, as it requires an approach that questions our thoughts, experiences and actions. This enables us to learn from experience and enhances our knowledge and skills. The important point is that through reflection as social workers we can change how we think, feel and behave to better meet the needs of service users and carers.

Where do we start?

Assessment is a fundamental process in social work and requires the development of critical thinking skills, which Cottrell (2005, p2) defines as a process that incorporates:

- having the ability to recognise other people's view points and their reasons for maintaining this perspective;
- being able to evaluate the evidence to support a particular view;
- having the capacity to compare and contrast different arguments;
- being able to consider issues in some depth and not just accept superficial explanations;

- having the skill to notice when arguments are used to support a particular position that appear sound but are in fact erroneous;

- being able to reflect in a structured manner;

- having the capacity to bring together different factors and come to a conclusion;

- being able to present a well-evidenced argument that is credible to other people.

Cottrell suggests that sometimes our emotional responses can impact in an unhelpful way on our capacity to think critically. Therefore, if we learn how to recognise and manage our emotions, for example if we are aware that certain situations will affect us, we can better understand why we feel a particular way, and we can learn how to manage these feelings through thinking about them critically. The experience of Josh, a student social worker, illustrates this.

CASE STUDY

As part of Josh's first practice placement he was allocated the role of link social worker with the local infant school. On his first visit it was raining heavily outside. The deputy headteacher greeted him warmly and showed him around the school. When they went through the cloakroom where all the children's wet coats hung, Josh became over-whelmed with feelings of fear and anxiety. He felt confused and embarrassed about his feelings, and hoped that the deputy headteacher was not aware of his fear. It was as if he was five years old again. Josh had been bullied by three older boys in the cloakroom, which was some distance from the classrooms. He always tried to avoid using it, but when it was raining his teacher told him to hang his coat up. It was the smell of the wet coats that brought the memory back of something that had occurred 14 years earlier.

Parker and Bradley (2007) add to Cottrell's ideas by the inclusion of values and issues of diversity. They cite Sutton's ASPIRE model to represent the assessment process as a complete activity.

- **AS** –assessment

- **P** – Planning

- **I** – Intervention

- **RE** – Review and evaluation

This model is a good starting point to assess our learning and developmental needs, and then for us to reflect on how we might meet these needs through developing an action plan that builds on our experiences and the acquisition of knowledge and skills. Finally we can review the plan to see how effective it has been, and make appropriate changes. It is important to remember that all assessments are undertaken within a value base, and that as social workers a commitment to the values of equality and social justice are important, whether we are assessing other people's needs or our learning needs.

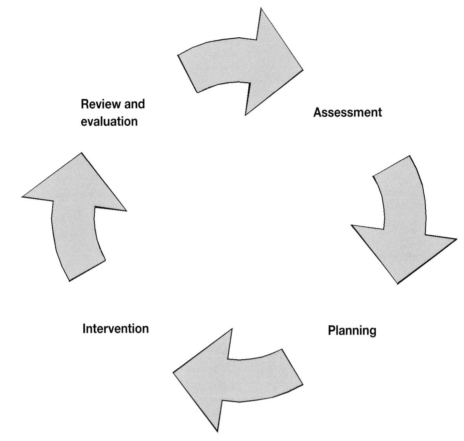

Figure 4.1 The ASPIRE model

Source: Sutton, C (2006) *Helping families with troubled children*. 2nd edition. © John Wiley & Sons Limited.
Reproduced with permission.

Approaches to self-assessment

There are a number of approaches that can be used to assess ourselves in terms of our
personality traits and preferred learning style. Strengths, weaknesses, opportunities and
threats (SWOT) analysis is a technique that is often used in organisations and teams to
take a position statement of how the organisation or team are functioning. This is an
extremely effective technique to use on ourselves (Thompson, 2006).

Suzy is a social work student and she completed this SWOT analysis to share with her practice assessor Nasreen at her practice placement in a family centre.

Suzy has been very honest in her self-analysis and shown that she has given it considerable
thought. She was congratulated by Nasreen for being prepared to really look at her developmental needs, so they could develop an action plan that set out how Suzy's learning
needs in the placement would be met.

Strengths	Weaknesses
I'm friendly and find it easy to get on with people	I have a tendency to worry and experience stress. (The risk of harm has been identified as a factor for most of the children I will be working with.)
I enjoy being with children	I am unsure if I will be able to manage emotionally in this placement. I get very upset when children are not treated affectionately
I want to support parents to care for their children, so that their life together is happier	I want people to like me, sometimes social workers have to make very difficult decisions, such as recommending that children be separated from their families
I am committed to working as a social worker, and motivated to learn and develop	At times I take myself and life a bit too seriously – I need to remember to have a sense of humour!
I always work hard	
I care about people and social justice	
Opportunities	**Threats**
To learn new skills and develop knowledge	Find that I can't cope with the work due to being upset and getting very stressed
Practise the skills and implement the theories learnt on my social work course at university	My fear of failure
Tackle my Weaknesses above and Threats opposite!	I don't have a lot of confidence in situations of conflict I set very high standards for myself, maybe they are not always realistic

Figure 4.2 Suzy's SWOT analysis at the start of her placement in a family centre

ACTIVITY 4.1

Do a SWOT analysis of yourself. It is important to be honest in the same way that Suzy has been. We will return to your SWOT analysis after Activity 4.2, by which time you will have made an assessment of yourself, which you may find very illuminating.

Comment

When tackling this exercise it will help you to use the template of four boxes. Do not try to do it in logical sequence, unless this is easiest for you. You may get more down by writing what first comes to you. You may find that what feels like a potential threat is also an opportunity, and so needs to go into both boxes.

RESEARCH SUMMARY

Research into the positive effects of writing has been shown by Pennebaker et al. (cited by Nicolson et al. (2006) and Bolton (2001). Duncan and Sheffield's (2005) research found that students who wrote in an unstructured manner in fact experienced increased levels of anxiety in contrast to students who did not write at all. This may relate to people ruminating and dwelling on difficulties through recording them. It is therefore suggested that the template set out below is used as this provides a process to problem-solve as well as reflect on issues (Nicolson et al., 2006, p85).

Structure for a reflective journal

Stage 1 – Reflecting on an issue or concern that you have. This should be done in an unstructured manner to capture your thoughts spontaneously.

Stage 2 – Analyse what you have written and ask yourself the following questions:

- What is going on here?

- What assumptions am I making?

- What does this tell me about my beliefs?

- Are there other ways of looking at this?

Be precise and specific in your analysis – paraphrase the key points. If you read your journal over a number of entries are there any themes emerging?

Stage 3 – Action Answer the following questions:

- What action can I take?

- How can I learn this?

- Would I respond differently if this occurs again?

- What does this tell me about the beliefs that I hold about myself?

This is an example of a journal entry that Suzy took to supervision.

I was sitting with Katie (19 years old) and her daughter Amy (nine months), who was on her lap. Amy spilt her drink over her and Katie.

*Katie got very angry really quickly and shouted at Amy: 'You f****** dirty cow – you've messed up your new dress. Get the f**** off me.'*

*She then roughly put Amy on the floor. Amy started to cry, and this made Katie even more angry. She told her to 'shut the f**** up.'*

I watched and I froze. I was very frightened. Katie's anger was so quick. I hate myself for being frightened. I'm pathetic, useless, weak. I can't cope. I just sat and watched.

(continued)

CASE STUDY continued

Colleen (staff) heard the shouting and came in. She picked Amy up and gave her a cuddle, and sat near Katie. She asked Katie what had happened. Katie said that Lee (her boyfriend) has been seeing her best friend, and Amy spilling her drink was the last straw.

Colleen listened to Katie and when she had calmed down, she talked with her about the effect her outburst had had on Amy. Finally Katie took Amy from Colleen and told Amy that she was sorry that she had taken her anger out on her. Colleen discussed with Katie age-appropriate behaviour and that children do mess their clothes up. She offered to help Katie learn how to manage her frustration and angry feelings.

Following this incident I had a headache, and my shoulders felt sore where I had tensed them. I also felt really down.

Analysis

When I analysed this I became aware of how I behave under stress and what I tell myself. This is a summary of the key learning points for me.

- I froze with fear

- I was frightened (although at no time did I feel threatened)

- I thought 'I hate myself for not protecting or comforting Amy'

- I told myself 'I am useless, pathetic and weak'

- I remember thinking 'I can't cope'

- My shoulders and neck feel sore, and I had a headache

- When I think about the incident now I feel sad.

Action

1. To get better management of my thoughts and feelings, and to discuss with Nasreen ways that I can begin to do this.

2. To discuss with Nasreen offering to work jointly with Colleen to support Katie to understand Amy's needs, and manage her angry feelings. (Colleen will be a good role model.)

ACTIVITY 4.2

Now let us return to you, and the SWOT analysis that you completed earlier.

- *What did your SWOT analysis reveal about you?*

- *What are your strengths?*

- *How might you build on them and could this impact on areas that you have identified as weaknesses?*

Comment

Start to write a reflective journal using the structure outlined above. Remember to think about actions that you could take to solve any problems or issues that you have. Try to get into the habit of doing this. You might want to take a notebook with you and jot down thoughts and observations that you have during the day, and then explore them in more detail in your reflective journal.

Planning

In the same way that an assessment of service users or carers enables social workers to develop a care plan to meet people's needs, so the assessment that Suzy has completed through the SWOT analysis, reflective journal and supervision with Nasreen has identified her learning needs.

They identified self-management in relation to stress as one of Suzy's priorities. Together they reformulated this into a positive goal that focuses on what Suzy wants, to be personally effective in her practice, rather than emphasising what she does not want – excessive stress.

This is the action plan that has been produced. Do note that part of the plan requires Suzy to use her own learning to enable service users and carers to manage stressful feelings, and thoughts which may then be manifested in behaviour as evidenced by Katie's outburst.

Suzy's action plan
Student Social Worker: Suzy Fitzgerald

Practice Assessor: Nasreen Khan

Aims

- *This action plan seeks to enhance Suzy's personal effectiveness as a student social worker at Southside Family Centre.*

Objectives

- *To support Suzy to develop strategies and approaches that enable her to reduce unhelpful stress that impacts on her work within the Centre, especially in relation to conflict.*

- *For Suzy to use her own self-development to support children and parents at the Centre to manage stressful and unhelpful thoughts, feelings and behaviours.*

- *For Suzy to develop her capacity to take personal responsibility for her own continuous professional development and become a reflective practitioner.*

Actions

- *Suzy to write a reflective journal using the agreed structure and bring a journal extract to supervision every week for discussion.*

(continued)

> ## Suzy's action plan continued
>
> - *Suzy to do some research into the fight or flight theory for discussion in supervision. (This will be linked to university work.)*
> - *Suzy will reflect on the use of cognitive and behavioural theories in terms of herself. (This will be linked to university work.)*
> - *Nasreen to give Suzy information about breathing, neck and shoulder exercises.*
> - *The learning from the above to be taught to service users and carers focusing initially on joint work between Suzy and Colleen with Katie.*
>
> ### Outcomes
>
> - *The learning that Suzy achieves in terms of the management of her own responses to stress can be used with families at the Centre, many of whom experience significant stress.*
>
> ### Review
>
> - *The action plan will be discussed at supervision each week in terms of progress.*
> - *A full review will take place in six weeks' time.*

The action plan requires Suzy to research into particular theories such as fight or flight, as well as learning physical exercises to manage stress. The cumulative effect of stress, over many years, has serious consequences for people's health and well-being. Learning breathing exercises (Baylis, cited in Linley and Joseph, 2004) has a beneficial effect on slowing the heart rate and calming the nervous system. Butler and Hope (2007) provide accessible and extensive information about relaxation exercises, as well as many other approaches to manage your emotions, thoughts and behaviour.

It is important to become aware of how you are reacting physically. So you can change your position to reduce the muscles becoming rigid. Once you do become conscious of your body, the ability to reduce physical tension will enable you to feel mentally calmer; although it is important to remember that sometimes your body may be alerting you to genuine risks.

Approaches that can help us manage our stress

As well as developing an understanding of the fight or flight theory, Suzy needs to become aware of her self-talk, and assess what this tells her about the beliefs she holds about herself. We will also consider the role that cognitive and behavioural theories can play.

If Suzy is able to integrate her understanding of these theories into her practice, it will assist her in her goal to be personally effective in her work with the families attending the family centre. Additionally she will be able to explain these approaches to the families, so together they can work on bringing about changes that will ameliorate some of the difficulties that they are experiencing.

Fight or flight theory

Goleman (1996) explains the fight or flight theory as a physiological response to situations where we believe ourselves to be in danger. Our minds think that we are about to be attacked and our bodies tense ready to either attack the perceived aggressor or run away. This response dates back to prehistoric times when human beings had to respond to many physical threats in the same way that animals do. The difficulty is that we can respond to situations in an automatic physiological manner that is disproportionate to the threat that we are experiencing.

If we return to Suzy's reflective journal, she has written:

- I froze with fear.

- I was frightened (although at no time did I feel threatened).

- I have become aware of how often my shoulders and neck feel sore and I often get headaches.

- When I think about the incident I feel sad.

In this situation Suzy's automatic physiological response was to sense danger, and she became immobilised rather like the proverbial frightened rabbit that stops in the middle of the road as a car approaches rather than run to safety. Suzy's body has tensed, especially around her shoulders and neck, which has probably resulted in her getting a headache.

If Suzy had slowed her breathing, lowered her shoulders and her self-talk had been encouraging and reassuring this might have prevented her reaction.

Belief systems

Our minds are constantly full of thoughts and ideas (self-talk) which we discuss with ourselves. Sometimes our thoughts are positive and helpful while at other times they are destructive and problematic. The quality of our self-talk reveals what we believe about ourselves. Beliefs may or may not have any objective truth; they are quite simply what we believe to be true. In childhood we develop beliefs that are 'so fundamental and deep' that we do not express them to ourselves or others (Beck, 1995, p15). Often we are not even aware of what they are. Children who have experienced harsh or unfair criticism about a particular behaviour that has been generalised may grow up with non-affirming self-beliefs.

Suzy's self-talk is very negative and unsupportive:

- I hate myself

- I am pathetic, useless and weak

- I can't cope.

If we look at these statements in more detail they suggest that Suzy is always pathetic, useless, weak and unable to cope in all situations and at all times. This is factually untrue and has impacted on her self-esteem and confidence. It has affected her mood. Suzy wrote in her reflective journal how she feels sad when she thinks about the incident with Katie and Amy.

ACTIVITY 4.3

By starting to take notice of your thoughts you will be able to assess if your self-talk is critical and chiding like Suzy's or positive, supportive and enabling.

What do you say to yourself during times of stress? Whose voice is speaking – yours or a critical teacher or parent? Do you tell yourself I can't cope with one more thing to do *or* I can do this *when the going gets tough?*

Keep a record in your reflective journal of the thoughts and images that go through your mind.

Comment

Can you identify any patterns emerging? Can you relate your thoughts to changes in mood such as suddenly feeling irritated because you have remembered a task that you have to do, or feeling excited when you think of an anticipated pleasurable event such as going on holiday?

Cognitive behaviour therapy

During the 1960s Aaron T Beck developed cognitive behaviour therapy, which was directed towards assisting people to solve their difficulties through restructuring their thought processes. Beck trained as a psychotherapist and found that traditional psychodynamic interventions took people back to early experiences where they gained insights into the possible causes of their difficulties, but did not enable them to necessarily overcome them. Beck developed an approach that was fixed in the present and that challenged dysfunctional thinking and behaviour.

If we consider Suzy's self-talk and how this reinforces her beliefs about herself we can see how these thoughts are problematic and in fact increase her stress, and impact on her feelings, behaviour and physiology. This can be expressed in a diagram (adapted from Beck, 1995, p18) as seen in Figure 4.3.

Rational emotive behaviour therapy

Albert Ellis (1955) developed this therapeutic intervention which emphasises that people need to have a purpose and goals to achieve if their lives are to be satisfying. This can be undermined by irrational thoughts that prevent people achieving their goals. Ellis developed the ABC schema as a tool to challenge dysfunctional beliefs and thoughts. It operates as follows:

A = **Adversity** the situation that triggered the belief

B = **Belief** the person holds

C = **Consequence** the emotional, behavioural and physiological impact of the belief.

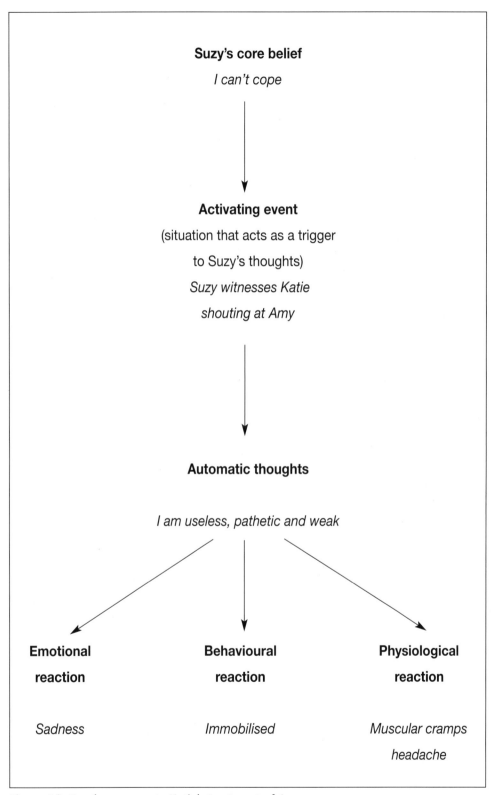

Figure 4.3 Suzy's response to Katie's treatment of Amy

We often think that an event (adversity) happens and this causes us to feel or behave in a particular way. In fact it is our belief about the cause of the event that makes us feel and behave as we do. Below is an example of how the approach works.

CASE STUDY

Paul has completed his BA in Social Work and has applied for a vacancy in the team where he had his final placement. He is very confident that he will be offered a permanent job, as his practice assessor has been very positive about his performance.

Paul contacts his personal tutor Winston at university following the interview and tells him: 'I am devastated, Winston, I didn't get the job. I don't understand. I feel really bad. It's shattered my confidence. Can I come and see you please?'

Winston meets with Paul and they agree to structure their discussion around the ABC approach at Winston's suggestion.

Adversity – Paul is not offered the post in the community mental team where he had his last practice placement as a student.

Consequence – Paul explains that he feels very upset and thinks that maybe the team do not like him, and that his practice is poor.

Winston points out that Paul has gone from the situation of not being offered the job to the consequences. In other words Paul thinks he feels depressed because he did not get the job. In fact it is Paul's beliefs about not getting the job that have caused his depression. Winston asks him to explain what goes through his mind when he thinks about not being offered the job.

Paul says: 'I feel I am rubbish. I was there for a 100 days and I was OK as a student but they won't employ me. Maybe they don't like me, but I liked them. It was a great placement.'

Winston repeats back to Paul what he has said: 'I feel I am rubbish.' Winston writes down the following with Paul:

Adversity

• *I have not been offered a job in the team where I had my last placement.*

Belief

• *I am rubbish.*

Consequences

• *I feel depressed.*

Winston suggests Paul should put forward arguments that dispute his self-belief that he is rubbish. Paul could do this by imagining a supportive friend is pointing out all his strengths, or he has a lawyer arguing his case for him.

CASE STUDY continued

Disputation

Paul was able to think of the following:

- *I have achieved my BA in Social Work and I am now qualified*

- *I work hard: this can be evidenced by the tutors' comments on my third-year dissertation*

- *Feedback from the service users' group that I developed in my last placement about my role as the group facilitator was very positive*

- *The manager in the hospice where I had my first placement told me that the multi-disciplinary team had so enjoyed having a social work student on placement, that they would like to take another student from this university.*

Winston advises Paul that telling himself that he is rubbish was an example of negative thinking. In addition Paul had generalised about himself, blamed himself, personalised the situation and had tried to mind-read the interviewing panel. For example, Paul assumed that maybe they did not like him. Winston suggested that Paul should turn negative thoughts into positive thinking habits, as he was creating for himself considerable stress by his critical and harsh attitude towards himself.

They then moved on to consider some options that Paul could pursue to learn from the experience, and plan for the future. Seligman (2002, p93) has added Energisation and Disputation to the ABC approach. This enabled Paul to set himself some tasks, and challenge his negative thinking.

Energisation

- *I will contact the Chair of the interviewing panel and ask for feedback as to why I was not offered the job.*

- *I will take notes from this conversation and use these as a basis of an action plan. (I know that I did not sufficiently address issues about equalities in the case study, and that I could have shown more awareness about the impact of policy on local mental health services.)*

- *I will meet with the careers officer in the university and ask for some support in preparing for interviews.*

- *I will work hard on developing positive thinking habits – this is important for me personally, but also in my work with service users and carers.*

Returning to the family centre, we will see how Colleen and Suzy worked with Katie using this approach.

CASE STUDY

Katie has been attending the family centre for three weeks. During that time she has been able to discuss with Colleen and Suzy her sense of hopelessness, and her expectation that Amy will be removed from her care. She has spoken about being angry with the whole world, and suspects that this is linked to the death of her mother three years ago. She knows that sometimes she speaks harshly to Amy, and then feels guilty afterwards. Using the ABC approach they worked through with Katie the incident where Amy had spilt her drink. This is set out as a conversation between Katie and Colleen (see Figure 4.4).

Adversity	Colleen	Katie, what was going through your mind before Amy spilt her drink?
	Katie	*I had this picture of Lee with Sarah, who is meant to be my best friend, going out together. I thought about Mum and about how lonely I am.*
Belief	Colleen	Tell me more about your lonely feelings Katie.
	Katie	*Mum was 38, when she died. I often think if she had really loved me she wouldn't have died. I know it's daft because she died of cancer. Amy's father never bothered with me and now Lee has gone.*
	Colleen	Katie are you saying that you feel unloved and no one will ever love you?
	Katie	*I suppose I am.*
Consequences	Katie	*I get stressed out and angry about stupid things that don't matter, like Amy messing her clothes up.*
Disputation	Colleen	Katie, it must be hard for you to cope with the belief that you are unlovable. Even if it were true it's important that you accept yourself. Another way of thinking about this is: *I'm my own person and I can love myself, so I will always be loved. This will make me more attractive to other people, as I will feel good about myself.*
Energisation	Colleen	Katie, do you think it would help to start to notice what goes through your mind when you are upset, or feel down? Bad moods don't just happen, there is always something that causes them. Then you can start to challenge some of those self-beliefs you have. I can show you some breathing exercises and ways of relaxing physically, as that will help too. The other thing is that we have links with the college. We could look to see if there is a course that you might be interested in. It would enable you to make new friends.
	Katie	*I am already starting to think more about things. I want to be good to Amy. You are right, I have always managed on my own. I would like you to teach me how to relax. I think I've been low for so long it's got to be a habit, but I feel much better now. It helps to talk about things – you help me to see things from a different point of view.*

Figure 4.4 Katie and Colleen's conversation

From Colleen's conversation with Katie we can see the impact that unfounded beliefs and negative thinking habits can have emotionally, behaviourally and physiologically for Katie, and importantly for Amy too. For Katie and Suzy the process of reflecting and having the opportunity to talk through their insights is necessary for Katie to develop into a consistently caring parent, and for Suzy as a social worker.

ACTIVITY **4.4**

Think of a situation that has caused you anxiety and upset. Analyse it using the ABC approach. Reflect on your understanding of the situation now. What have you learnt about your beliefs?

Comment

The ABC approach is very effective in enabling us to gain new insights into problems, and assists us to challenge ideas and beliefs that cause us difficulties. It is essential to remember that it is often not the actual event that causes us distress, but our reaction to it. If you recall, Josh became panicky when he smelt the wet coats in the cloakroom. It triggered a memory of being bullied by other children. In reality Josh was now an adult and in no danger from ever being bullied again in an infant school cloakroom.

Critique of the theory

Milner and O'Byrne (2002) state that cognitive and behavioural theories view change as required at an individual level rather than taking account of societal inequalities. In addition the structured approach of the intervention can feel mechanistic and prescriptive, locating the difficulty in the person, rather than taking account of their social environment and experiences. Katie's situation is not understood, for example, from a feminist perspective. This would place emphasis on her as a lone parent operating within a patriarchal social system that expects her to assume care of Amy without similar requirements of Amy's father. In other words, if she had deserted Amy as her father had, this would be viewed more harshly because Katie is a woman and mother. It can of course be argued that by enabling Katie to develop the capacity of accepting herself, she will be able to dispute negative self-beliefs, which would enhance her well-being and empower her.

Review and evaluation

In terms of Suzy's movement through the ASPIRE cycle we can see that she is in the process of professional and personal development and change.

- Through the SWOT analysis she has assessed her strengths and areas for development.

- Suzy is now keeping a structured reflective journal.

- She is working on developing positive thinking habits through monitoring her self-talk, developing an understanding of cognitive behaviour therapy and the ABC technique.

- Suzy is co-working with an experienced member of staff (Colleen) with a view to using her as a role model in order to develop her own practice.

- Finally Suzy is committed to integrating her learning into her practice, and sharing this knowledge and skills within her work with service users and carers.

These activities and approaches will be reviewed and evaluated with her practice assessor, but it is important that Suzy takes personal responsibility for her own learning and development.

C H A P T E R   S U M M A R Y

In this chapter we have explored the use of self-assessment as a vehicle to start to develop reflective practice. Cognitive and behavioural theories have been the dominant theoretical perspective examined, with an emphasis on its practical application for service users, carers and social workers. It is necessary to consider what approaches work for us prior to utilising them on service users and carers. Our commitment and optimism in our capacity to support people in the process of development and change lie in being able to reflect on our own beliefs, motivations and actions, and the development of positive thinking habits. If we can believe in our capacity to change and develop we then can help others to do so too.

FURTHER READING

Butler, G and Hope, T (2007) *Manage your mind*. 2nd edition. Oxford: Oxford University Press.
This is an excellent book that addresses all aspects of developing well-being, and is written in an accessible manner. It includes many helpful approaches to combating self-doubt and enhancing self-esteem.

Seligman, M (2003) *Authentic happiness*. London: Nicholas Brealey Publishing.
This book promotes the study of positive psychology rather than pathology. It provides evidence of how we can become more optimistic and positive in our outlook, thereby enhancing our own happiness and that of those around us.

Chapter 5

Listening to carers and service users

Andy Mantell

ACHIEVING A SOCIAL WORK DEGREE

This chapter will help you to achieve the following National Occupational Standards.

Key Role 1: Prepare for, and work with individuals, families, carers, groups and communities to assess their needs and circumstances

1.1 Review case notes and other relevant literature

1.2 Liaise with others to access additional information that can inform initial contact and involvement.

1.3 Evaluate all information to identify the best form of initial involvement

2.1 Inform individuals, families, carers, groups and communities about your own, and the organisation's duties and responsibilities

2.2 Work with individuals, families, carers, groups and communities to identify, gather, analyse and understand information

2.3 Work with individuals, families, carers, groups and communities to enable them to analyse, identify, clarify and express their strengths, expectations and limitations

2.4 Work with individuals, families, carers, groups and communities to enable them to assess and make informed decisions about their needs, circumstance, risks, preferred options and resources

3.1 Assess and review the preferred options of individuals, families, groups and communities

3.2 Assess needs, risks and options taking into account legal and other requirements

3.3 Assess and recommend an appropriate course for individuals, families, carers, groups and communities

Key Role 2: Plan, carry out, review and evaluate social work practice, with individuals, families, carers, groups, communities and other professionals

4.1 Assess the urgency of requests for action

4.3 Plan and implement action to meet the immediate needs and circumstances

4.4 Review the outcomes with individuals, families, carers, groups, communities, organisations, professionals and others

5.1 Develop and maintain relationships with individuals, families, carers, groups, communities and others

5.2 Work with individuals, families, carers, groups, communities and others to avoid crisis situations and address problems

6.4 Review the effectiveness of the plans with the people involved

6.5 Renegotiate and revise the plans to meet changing needs and circumstances

Key Role 3: Support individuals to represent their needs, views and circumstances

10.1 Assess whether you should act as an advocate for the individuals, families, carers, groups and community.

10.2 Assist individuals, families, carers, groups and communities to access independent advocates

19.4 Critically reflect upon your own practice and performance using supervision and support systems. It will also introduce you to the following academic standards as set out in the social work subject benchmark statements:

3.1.1 Social work services and service users
The nature and validity of different definitions of and explanations for, the characteristics and circumstances of service users and the services required by them

3.1.5 The nature of social work practice
The process of reflection and evaluation, including familiarity with a range of approaches for evaluating welfare outcomes, and their significance for the development of practice and practitioners.

Introduction

This chapter will explore reflective practice, with a particular emphasis on the importance of integrating the perspectives of carers and people who use services, which will be an important part of your social work training. Consequently, the chapter starts with an exploration of the contentious nature of these often taken-for-granted terms and continues to explore these issues throughout.

The experiences of families of people with Huntington's disease are drawn upon to highlight the competing expectations of social work intervention which may be held by families, disabled people and practitioners. The chapter concludes with an exploration of how these expectations can influence the social worker's reflections on the nature and outcomes of their practice.

Huntington's disease is a rare neuro-degenerative condition, which carries a 50 per cent possibility of inheritance from an affected parent. Familial 'carers' can be faced with managing cognitive, motor and behavioural disorders, whilst uncertain about their own at-risk status. Onset usually occurs from the late 30s to the mid-50s and life expectancy is approximately 15–20 years.

Telling a story

Reflecting, as you have seen in Chapter 2, can be viewed as telling a story. In the process of constructing that narrative you are making sense of complex situations and your role within those circumstances. In social work this is not simply a contemplative narrative. Social sciences seek to understand social phenomena, but social work also seeks to intervene (Johnsson and Svensson, 2004). Your reflection is therefore purposeful, forming a critical aspect of improving your practice.

Social work intervention has been divided by Parker and Bradley (2010) into four stages: assessment, planning, intervention and review (ASPIRE). These stages have been expanded here to illuminate the accompanying reflective process. This consideration of reflection (also see Chapter 1) draws upon Schön's (1983) seminal work. In addition to reflection in action, i.e. your thinking at the time, and reflection on action, i.e. your thinking afterwards (Johnsson and Svensson, 2004), reflection before action is also essential.

One definition of reflection states: *a generic term for those intellectual and affective activities in which individuals engage to explore their experiences in order to lead to new understandings and appreciations* (Boud and Knights, 1996, p19). Whilst Schön (1983) considered some of this process as *beyond conscious articulation*, reflection is viewed here as a lifelong journey to uncover your motivations for actions and so be able to consciously influence and justify your practice. As such, reflective practice must be experienced rather than abstractly taught.

Naming the characters

The language that we employ to tell a story shapes the images and interpretations that are produced. The main protagonists in this story are called 'carers' and 'people who use services'.

ACTIVITY **5.1**

What's in a name?

Write down what the terms 'carers' and 'people who use services' mean to you.

Write down what these terms imply to you.

Write down your expectations of a 'carer'.

Write down your expectations of 'a person who uses services'.

Now think of a time that you received care from another person. Did you think of that person as a 'carer' and yourself as an actual or potential 'person who uses services'?

Comment

We tend to think about care in terms of the relationships within which it occurs (Morris, 1993). The term 'carer' was hardly used before the 1970s and it encompasses a range of meanings. The carers' movement has striven for recognition and support of the caring role undertaken by families, whilst the independent living movement has questioned the assumption of receiving care from the family (Morris, 1993).

Caring can imply emotional care (Thomas, 1993), i.e. caring about (Parker, 1981) someone, and instrumental care (Thomas, 1993), i.e. caring for them (Parker, 1981). People tend to view 'caring for' as synonymous with 'caring about'. This dominant perspective can influence family members providing and receiving care (Mantell, 2006), an inability to provide physical care becoming misconstrued as a negative reflection upon the love between two individuals. Family, friends, neighbours and professionals also imbued with this perspective may provide additional pressure upon family members to care. In some cases if one family member assumes or is given responsibility, it can assuage the potential obligation of others.

This expectation of care within relationships is enshrined within the Department of Health's (1990) community care policy guidance definition of a carer:

A person who is not employed to provide the care in question by any body in the exercise of its function under any enactment. Normally, this will be a person who is looking after another adult in the home who is frail, ill and/or mentally or physically disabled, and where the dependency relationship exceeds that implicit in normally dependent relationships between family members *(Department of Health 1990: Appendix B/1 Glossary).*

Note how this definition demonstrates how 'carer' is a relational term. For there to be a carer there must be a cared-for person. In the Department of Health's (1990) definition the latter is defined by their weakness; as frail, for example, and their relationship is defined as one of dependency. This oversimplified, static relationship denies the carer weakness and the cared-for person strength. It ignores the complexity and richness of relationships (Schofield, 1998). You may have mentioned something like this in your responses to Activity 5.1.

This Department of Health (1990) definition formally sanctions this correlation of labour with love, but also indicates that there is a point where this can be exceeded and at this point the person becomes a carer. The criterion for becoming a carer is therefore where customary expectations are exceeded (Schofield, 1998). However, whilst those members of the public whose expectations are exceeded will soon be informed by social workers of their organisation's criteria for providing support, other relatives may not conceive of any point where their expectation could be exceeded.

In social work the term 'client' has fallen from favour; it developed negative connotations and became viewed as stigmatising. It was replaced with the term 'service user' and more recently with the term 'people who use services'. However, do people actually prefer this term?

ACTIVITY 5.2

*Who are you calling a ******?*

The language we use can cause offence. What name would you prefer to be called: 'service user', 'person who uses services', 'client' or 'customer'?

Think of a new term that encompasses what you would like the word to portray.

Comment

The term 'customer' does not accurately encompass the range of interactions between social workers and the public. It seems a particularly inappropriate reference to apply to the statutory aspects of the social worker's role, for example, the compulsory detention of a mentally disordered person under the Mental Health Act 2007.

The phrase 'people who use services' reduces the potential association of 'service user' with the term 'user', which has been negatively employed to refer to people who misuse substances. This new term conforms to the People First movement's eponymous doctrine of not losing sight of the person, but at the cost of becoming unwieldy. Ironically, it risks being reduced to the even more dehumanising acronym PWUS. At the same time, 'people who use services' defines the individual by the services that they use and consequently perpetuates the view of them as dependent, rather than empowered. As a term it still fails to adequately reflect the subtleties of the social worker's involvement with people, instead perhaps tellingly, focusing on the resource outcome of involvement. It will be interesting to see how this language is affected by the implementation of the personalisation agenda.

RESEARCH SUMMARY

Morris (1993) found that disabled people receiving care from a family member referred to them as 'mother', etc. They talked about their relationships not about their carers (Morris, 1993, p154). Mantell (2006), in a qualitative study of carers for people with Huntington's disease, found that relatives in the early stages of providing care initially used the same terms, but over time the relationship could change to become dominated by care. In these circumstances spouses valued and felt empowered by viewing themselves as carers.

'People who use services' and 'carers' are the dominant terms used within social care and are consequently adopted here. However, it must be remembered that these contentious terms may have limited or no relevance to those with whom we work.

Governing variables

Schön (1983) identified that practice is framed by a range of governing variables, which act as limiting factors upon your practice. Legislation, the policies and procedures of employers, instructions from managers, the GSCC code of practice and the practitioner's own values and ethics all set the parameters within which your interventions occur. In order to empower, and engender trust from, people who use services and carers it is essential to be open and honest about what you can do.

Pre-assessment

Before you undertake a visit you will need to gather as much information as possible. This is an initial step towards understanding what is going on, a first tentative telling of the story, reflection before action. It is as much hypothetical as fact, questions to be tested when the visit occurs. It is a telling of the anticipated story that is likely to be clouded by governing variables, such as procedures, and your previous experiences of similar situations. This enables you to identify which of your skills and knowledge may be applicable and/or need developing and potential weaknesses in past practice to guard against. You are therefore reflecting on the potential limitations of the transferability of skills and knowledge from previous practice to this new situation (Gould, 2004). What skills and knowledge do you need to develop and what mistakes guard against? This forms part of your ongoing learning process in which you question how emotionally and practically prepared you feel for the unique challenges that you will face.

Huntington's disease is illustrative of numerous rare conditions where workers may lack knowledge. Carers and people who used services found that some professionals proactively sought information; however, others relied on the carers' knowledge. This could add to the responsibilities upon carers and leave them anxious that there might be key information that they do not know (Mantell, 2006).

Other professionals tried to hide their lack of knowledge behind overt displays of being an expert or relying on their usual procedures, leaving carers angry and frustrated (Mantell, 2006). Refusal to acknowledge their lack of knowledge undermined carers' confidence in professionals. In social work we are often in the situation of only holding partial knowledge and must be sensitive to its applicability and potential impact in any given situation.

Pre-plan and identify strategies

Pre-planning incorporates a further aspect of reflection before action, considering various scenarios and corresponding strategies to manage them. When I was a student social worker in a rural team I was asked by a GP to assess a person for attending a day centre. I couldn't drive and it took me two hours to get there, by which time it was snowing heavily. I knocked and introduced myself and said that I understood that he was interested in day care. He replied no and slammed the door shut. After several more unsuccessful attempts to engage him, I travelled the two hours back. I had gone armed with details of a range of day centres, but it had never occurred to me that I would receive such a blunt response. When I contacted the GP, he informed me that he hadn't discussed day care with the person, but just thought it might be a good idea.

This example illustrates the importance of checking referral information and the risk of giving too much weight to pre-planning. Pre-plans are at best hypotheses to be tested and agreed with the carer(s) and person who uses services. The expert model is particularly at risk of elevating the importance of the professionals' plans or ignoring the views and feelings of the carer(s) and the person who uses services.

Planning and identifying strategies is primarily an organic process evolving within interactions with agencies, people who use services and carers. Interventions need to be negotiated rather than pre-ordained, if people who use services and carers are to be empowered.

CASE STUDY

Making informed decisions

Cathy (all names have been changed to preserve confidentiality), aged 34, tested negative to carrying the Huntington's disease gene. She had a younger brother who committed suicide (before being aware of the family history of Huntington's disease). Cathy provided care for her mother who lived in a separate home, but following a fall her mother was admitted to hospital and deemed unable to care for herself or live alone any more. In her early 50s, her mother was admitted to a care home for older people. Cathy did not consider that either she or her mother were fully consulted in the process:

No, they didn't give me a choice at all. They just said you know we're sticking her in there, because they've got room. No, they didn't ask my opinion, and you know, all I mean, I was relieved. I just thought you know thank God for that. And it didn't occur to me to ask any questions like, did they know anything about Huntington's or anything like that.

(Mantell, 2006, p149)

(Care) home from home

What good practice steps do you think should be taken to enable a person to enter a care home?

Why do you think that in some situations, such as Cathy's, this good practice does not occur?

What do you think could be done to remedy these difficulties?

Comment

As well as highlighting the importance of engaging with people who use services and their carers to provide informed choices, Cathy's experiences also demonstrate how the level of choice for specialist provisions can be limited in crisis situations. Proactive planning, such as developing care pathways, is essential to facilitating real choices for people.

Assessment/intervention

Just seeing someone influences their situation: it may, for example, elicit guilt at their behaviour, relief and validation or high expectations that the situation will change (Mantell, 2006). Reflection in action forms an integral part of assessment. A comparison occurs between your expectation of the situation and the actual situation. This adjustment enables a better approximation of the carers and people who use services perspectives to evolve. The assessment may, for example, identify more pressing needs to be met than those previously anticipated. The practitioner has to be particularly sensitive to the ways in which their preconceived ideas can influence situations. Their assumptions can limit the interpretation of situations and deny individuals the space to express their feelings.

Language and assessment

As we have already seen, assumptions may stem from the language that we assume within professional cultures, for example, within the social care culture individuals within families are identified as carers or people who use services. Such perceptions can limit our understanding and inhibit our interventions.

Derived from the government's policy (Department of Health, 1990), social workers are concerned with the level of care, i.e. regular and substantial in considering if a person is a carer. In this quantification they focus on the instrumental care and can treat carers as care workers. The focus shifts to tasks they are undertaking and their ability to do those tasks. They may concentrate on issues such as training, for example, in manual handling or gaining carer's allowance. On one level such factors are essential, but they can also add to the professionalising (Henderson, 2001) of the carer. As Henderson (2001, p157) stated, being the expert on someone can have a devastating effect on their relationship. Care shifts from an element of their relationship to defining that relationship.

Community care is based on familial care before state intervention (Morris, 1993). The terms 'people who use services' and 'carer' when employed by social care services are not simply descriptive, they represent key concepts within community care. The person who uses services is the person whom state services will have to support if the family does not. It is perhaps not surprising that family members are therefore seen as synonymous with carers.

ACTIVITY **5.4**

Who cares?

Do you think that families should be expected to care for their members?

Would you expect a family member or partner to care for you? Would there be a limit to what you would expect or want them to do?

Do you think your expectations would affect your view of family members of people who use services who refuse to provide care?

Comment

Presumptions of care within relationships and attendant judgements that a person does not love their relative if they do not provide care place considerable pressure upon family members, and women in particular, to provide care. Such expectations owe more to the enduring myth of the prevalence of the idealised 'Oxo' family than the diverse reality of relationships. No account is taken of ambivalent or conflictual feelings that can exist within families.

CASE STUDY

Presumptive practice

Martha, aged 22, had a volatile relationship with her mother and had followed her sister's example in leaving home as soon as possible. She was, however, concerned that her mother was neglecting herself and despite arranging for her to attend a day centre and have a home help the situation continued to deteriorate. Martha and her elder sister were invited to a meeting at the day centre and were confronted by the spectacle of their mother being asked to perform tests in front of them to demonstrate that she was not well. As Martha pointed out she was well aware that her mother was not well and did not need her to be 'embarrassed' in this way.

Martha was then informed that her mother had Huntington's disease and: 'Oh, by the way, it is hereditary.' Whilst recovering from this shock the sisters were asked which one of them would look after their mother. Neither of them was in circumstances where they could look after their mother nor did they have the quality of relationship where they would want to provide that care.

It is very easy to become focused upon your own agenda and achieving your desired outcomes. Such practice becomes oblivious to the context in which interventions occur and the need to be sensitive to the impact of the process of intervention and the contestability of desired outcomes.

Services focus on burden of care, with the aim to support carers to care. This focus on burden has been highly criticised (Morris, 1993), for implying that the person being looked after is 'useless' or 'unproductive'. The term 'person who uses services' also risks perpetuating dependency. Whilst moving from the discredited term 'client', the person who uses services fails to denote a shift in the underlying cultural perspective, which persists in defining a disabled person in terms of receiving rather than managing their care.

Nolan (2001) argued that focusing on mutuality would be a better determinant of people being able to continue to manage than burden. Focusing on mutuality would not only identify if a primary motivator for caring still exists but also raises the ethical issue of whether people should be expected to provide care if their relationship has changed.

Familial obligation

In popular thought, care is associated with female traits and consequently the expectation of familial care is primarily one of female care. Qureshi and Simons (1987) in their *Hierarchy of obligation* identified how spouses were more likely to provide care than other family members; the next most likely were parents–adult children, and same household members were more likely to care than non-household members and that women are more likely to care than men. Such obligations are strongly defined by the cultural norms of those families, but can be inhibited by prejudice. Families with Huntington's disease, for example, face stigma, which can produce secrecy within the family (Mantell, 2006), denying relatives potential support.

This discussion illustrates how your perspectives on care are shaped by your social and professional culture. Even the language you use can limit your understanding of a situation and promote a particular agenda.

Plan and identify strategies

The core activity of planning and identifying strategies, requires reflection in action in order to maintain the necessary level of sensitivity to the preferences of all those involved.

Planning entails thinking about the future, which can be extremely empowering for some carers and people who use services, enabling them to gain a sense of control. However, for others, particularly families with degenerative diseases, planning means facing the future, which exposes their future loss. Consequently some carers, such as Tara, who cared for her husband, preferred to focus on the here and now:

> *I'd been a great believer, in fact, through Nigel's illness, I take one day at a time. I don't like, I can't think of the future, I don't like to think what the future may hold. I take one day at a time, I get up and just try and get through the day; if it's been a good day,*

good, and if it's been a bad day, then tomorrow might be better ... And that's how really I've coped with it. (Mantell, 2006, p215).

ACTIVITY 5.5

Looking to the future

What would be important to talk about with people who use services and their carers in such circumstances?

How would you feel about having such a conversation: would there be any topics that you would be nervous or uncomfortable about discussing, such as reduced sexual intimacy or death?

Comment

Your professional and personal perspectives can significantly influence how you explore the future with a person who uses services or carer. What is significant to you may not be as significant to them or it may hold a much greater significance. The dominance of the medical model can lead professionals to focus on the pathology of a condition. In contrast, carers focus on the individual affected by the condition, recognising their history, their character, their interests and their meaning to the carer. Equally the social taboo surrounding death in Western society can inhibit the person who uses services, carer and professional from exploring painful, but often necessary issues.

Intervention/Assessment

As you shift your focus towards intervention an ongoing element of assessment is essential. This includes a process of testing those pre-interview hypotheses that still appear applicable and also the generation and testing of new hypothesis. This process of reflection in action is concerned with ensuring that the understanding gained is and remains the best possible.

Reflection in action (see Chapter 1) is also focused upon the process: how are you interacting and understanding each other? What subtexts are occurring? This requires sensitivity to self as well as the others present, because communication may be at a non-verbal level. For example, a person who uses services who was depressed spoke to me in a calm quiet manner, but I felt uncomfortable, I was becoming tense. I realised that I was mirroring his tension, which was incongruent to his speech. Transference, i.e. of his tension, and counter-transference, i.e. my becoming tense, are psychoanalytical concepts which can help you to understand your interactions. They also highlight the origin of reflective practice in social work, as derived from its therapeutic tradition.

Reflection must also become outcome orientated: is the intervention still heading in the direction of the agreed objectives; if not, why not? Does it need to be redirected? Or do different objectives need to be identified? It is important not to confuse process and outcome;

for example, after being refused a package of care, a carer was told that the assessment was the service.

Outcome

The outcome of an intervention triggers reflection on action. This again focuses on both comparison of the outcome achieved with the outcome sought and consideration of the process: was it effective, could it be improved?

Review

A review can be seen as a formal process of reflection on action including all of the stakeholders. They enable the practitioners not only to confirm if the outcome has been successful, but also to reflect on how accurately the practitioners' views matched those of the person who uses services and carers and agencies involved.

The review may mark the end of a particular piece of practice or the start of further assessment of unmet needs. Regular reviews are particularly important when working with people with degenerative conditions such as Huntington's disease, where needs may change subtly over time. As Tom found when his wife first started showing symptoms of Huntington's disease:

> ... things creep up on you so gradually, things like for instance bottle tops being left undone, a slightly curious walk, the gait changes, the temper gets very slightly sharper, anybody who's experienced PMT would know exactly where we're coming from ... But it starts to multiply you see, and you think, is this right?

(Mantell, 2006, p181)

For the practitioner they are also ongoing audit points along with supervision, peer discussion and observation of their reflective process. Such external checks counter the potential neutral (Baldwin, 2004) or insular nature of an individual's reflections, promoting continued learning and development.

Reflection on action is about considering how you could have better achieved their objectives and your own. It may be about correcting mistakes or ways to improve and refine your practice. It is about learning from practice, which can be divided into two forms of learning. The first is single-loop learning (Argyris and Schön, 1996) and is where you tell the story again considering what you could have done differently to improve the process and outcome. The second is double-loop learning and is where you go further, to question the governing variables, for example challenging policy, as opposed to implementing them more effectively. For example, as a specialist local authority worker for people with acquired brain injury, I brought to my manager's attention that the eligibility criteria for disabled people did not include cognitive deficits and was therefore an inappropriate assessment tool for a wide range of people. Double-loop learning (see Chapters 8 and 9) requires organisations which encourage such thinking, in order to thrive (Baldwin, 2004).

Single-loop learning is more associated with students or newly qualified practitioners, as they understandably tend to adhere to rules. As you engage in post-qualifying training and develop your expertise, you will tend to incorporate double-loop learning and to integrate single- and double-loop learning into your reflections before and in practice. Expert practitioners also tend towards viewing rules more for guidance than obedience. This discretionary approach reduces insensitive organisational bureaucracy, but necessitates critical reflection to prevent 'street-level bureaucracy', i.e. idiosyncratic routines or prejudice aimed at reconciling the conflicting demands of organisations, people who use services and the practitioner's own value base (Lipsky, 1980).

ACTIVITY **5.6**

Professional discretion

In your practice setting how much discretion do you have?

How does this compare to your colleagues in other settings?

How does it compare to other professionals with whom you work?

What strategies do you adopt to avoid 'street-level bureaucracy'?

Comment

In the current managerial climate, emphasising quantifiable, evidence-based practice, it could be argued that professional leeway has been severely restricted (Johnsson and Svensson, 2004).

Understanding and desirable solutions

The model above is fine for providing a basic schematic of reflective practice. We tell the story to understand it better, which then informs our interventions. However, social work is a complex process. We have to be aware that there are multiple perspectives on a situation. Each party in the process has their own understanding of the situation and from that understanding flows their objectives and preferred solutions. For example, Karen cared for her husband, Ralph, but they had different views about how that care should be provided:

I might have been able to manage at home if he would be willing to have a nurse, or carers come in to help me. But he will not let them in the house.

(Mantell, 2006, p164)

ACTIVITY **5.7**

Who's right?

Whose rights should prevail in circumstances like those of Karen and Ralph?

Comment

In my experience, the views of the person who uses services tend to prevail in the short term, but if their carer reaches a point of being unable to continue, the person who uses services may find that they are admitted to a care home, in a crisis situation, with limited choices. Central to this undesired outcome is the level of capacity of the person who uses services. Huntington's disease, for example, can cause rigidity of thinking, limiting the person's ability to consider alternatives. Advanced planning may enable consensus to be achieved, but with some conditions such as dementia or acquired brain injury, the person may lack insight into their needs. The provisions of the Capacity Act 2005 have the potential to promote the views of the person who uses services, through advanced decisions to refuse treatment, but also to shift authority to the views of the carer, where the person who uses services' level of capacity is in doubt, through lasting powers of attorney, for example.

Social workers therefore need to develop a multi-sited understanding of a situation. That is a recognition that meaning is *constructed by multiple agents in varying contexts or places* (Marcus, 1998, p52). Social work's tendency to draw on a range of social sciences perhaps leaves social workers more sensitive to consider different approaches than may perhaps be the case if they came from a more defined tradition.

In working with families there is often an implicit assumption that consensus is achievable, but this may not be possible. In such circumstances, whose meanings and consequently objectives are we aiming to meet? A relative of a person who uses services who was a solicitor once said to me: Who is your client? I replied that they both were. She was identifying this potential conflict of interest. One of the criticisms of social work has been focusing on one family member's needs to the detriment of another's, for example, in Victoria Climbié's case.

Reflection is fundamentally about making the implicit explicit, in order to critically scrutinise practice. Practitioners need to recognise and value different people's objectives but be explicit about whose objectives are being prioritised and where appropriate to identify support or advocates for the other family members. This is not a straightforward process; at one point in practice one person's needs may be paramount but that can change over time. One solution would be for social workers to move from the terminology of 'carer' and 'person who uses services' and identify a 'primary client', who remains the focus of their intervention. As the shift to the personalisation agenda (DoH, 2007; DoH, 2008) proceeds, customers may demand that they become the primary focus. Already some people are demanding that level of demarcation. Clare, for example, called in a social worker when her husband developed auditory delusions, and believed that their neighbours were playing loud music.

And this social worker ... instead of her saying, now look Patrick there isn't any music ... she just said to him: 'Oh what type of music; classical, rock, country and western?' And I turned to her and I said: 'Well you're not helping at all.' I said: 'In fact, from what you've just said to him, you may as well go.' And I never had the woman again, I refused to have her, for the simple reason, she didn't help me at all, she was sort of backing him up.

ACTIVITY 5.8

Achieving outcomes
How would you have dealt with a situation like Clare's and Patrick's?

Comment

The outcome that Clare wanted was for the social worker to confirm to Patrick that he was imagining the music but also to support her. Patrick wanted the music to stop and to be taken seriously. The social worker in her attempt to engage with Patrick and gather more information (assessment) alienated Clare. Patrick appeared to be the social worker's primary client when Clare was assuming that *she* would be.

This illustration demonstrates the fragility of social work interventions. You may enter a person's home with a particular plan and a particular focus of your assessment, but your reflections before action have to be contrasted with your reflections in action. In this particular situation reflection on action would have been too late to alter this outcome.

C H A P T E R   S U M M A R Y

This chapter has highlighted the reflective process that coexists with social work practice. It has drawn on the example of people with Huntington's disease and their families to illustrate that the objectives of intervention are not always straightforward. Multi-sited meaning creates multi-sited objectives. Reflective practice enables social workers to develop the capacity for the creative (Trevithick, 2005) and discretionary practice to meet people's diverse demands. However, you need to be sensitive to uncovering your own agenda(s) and be explicit about whose objectives you are prioritising and the assumptions you may be making:

> *With care in the community of course, there's much more it being expected and assumed you're carers. And it's not always right. (Susan, who cared for her husband.)*

(Mantell, 2006, p177)

FURTHER READING

Cottrell, S (2005) *Critical thinking skills*. Basingstoke: Palgrave.
Excellent introductory text for developing your analytical skills.

Gould, N and Baldwin, M (eds) (2004) *Social work, critical reflection and the learning organisation*. Aldershot: Ashgate.
Slightly more advanced text on reflective practice in social work.

Gould, N and Taylor, I (eds) (1996) *Reflective learning for social work*. Aldershot: Ashgate.
Excellent introductory text to reflective practice in social work.

Parker, J and Bradley, G (2010) *Social work practice: Assessment, planning, intervention and review*. 3rd edition. Exeter: Learning Matters.
Read the original model, expanded upon within this chapter.

Chapter 6

Reflection and avoiding professional dangerousness

Sandra Wallis

A C H I E V I N G   A   S O C I A L   W O R K   D E G R E E

This chapter will help you meet the following National Occupational Standards.
Key Role 2: Plan, carry out, review and evaluate social work practice, with individuals, families, carers, groups, communities and other professionals
- Address behaviour which presents a risk to individuals, families, carers, groups and communities
Key Role 4: Manage risk to individuals, families, carers, groups, communities, self and colleagues
- Assess and manage risks to individuals, families, carers, groups and communities
- Assess, minimise and manage risk to self and colleagues
Key Role 6: Demonstrate professional competence in social work practice
- Research, analyse and use current knowledge of best social work practice
- Work within agreed standards of social work practice and ensure own professional development
- Contribute to the promotion of best social work practice
- Manage complex ethical issues, dilemmas and conflicts.
Achieving a post-qualifying social work award
This chapter will also assist you to evidence post-qualifying national criteria at the Specialist level:
(v) Use reflection and critical analysis to continuously develop and improve their specialist practice, including their practice in inter-professional and inter-agency contexts, draw systematically, accurately and appropriately on theories, models and relevant up-to-date research.
It will also introduce you to the following academic standards as set out in the subject benchmark statement:
3.1.5 Nature of social work practice
- Processes of reflection and evaluation including familiarity with a range of approaches for evaluating welfare outcomes, and their significance for the development of practice and the practitioner.

Introduction

This chapter was originally written in February 2007 at the same time as a highly critical report into the functioning of social care was published. This concerned the scandal surrounding the abuse of learning disabled service users in health settings (**www.cqc.org.uk**). It was the latest in a long line of reports that had highlighted dangerous instances within the social care sector where professionals involved had lost the sense of perspective in complex and challenging situations. Since then, another scandal has arisen, this time involving the abject failure of the social care force in regard to the abuse and subsequent death of a child in what has become known as the 'Baby P case' (www.dcsf.gov.uk/swtf). The dominant response to all the reports dealing with the deaths of children in child protection cases has been the rational bureaucratic one of developing the law, procedures and performance management in an attempt to avoid future catastrophes. In the process, attention to the psychological and emotional aspects of doing social work has been squeezed out. A feature of many of the reports is the many recorded instances where the failure of individual workers to carry out what seem to be quite simple tasks has contributed to the death of the child. There have been very few attempts at explaining these failures to act in terms of the feelings of the workers involved. To some extent, we in social work education have compounded this neglect with our emphasis on rights, and empower-ment and anti-oppressive practice without attending to what are the very real challenges of working with often aggressive and hostile involuntary clients – who do not want a service and make up a significant amount of statutory work.

The central purpose of this chapter is to improve our practice by reflecting on the feelings involved in our dealings with these and other families. In particular, the focus is on how to avoid acting in ways that can, albeit unintentionally, actually work so as to increase the risk of dangerousness. Such self-defeating practices have been grouped together under the term 'professional dangerousness'. Although these practices can occur within any area of social work, this part of the book will deal with the effect they have on child-protection work. An early comment from a fellow social work educator on the ideas behind this chapter was: *but I do not think that the concept of professional dangerousness will mean much to social work students and may actually be rather alarming and therefore off-put-ting to them.* My own view is that on the contrary it is important for social workers and students to be able to face up to and discuss, analyse and reflect upon the issue of dan-gerousness in our profession in order that it can be understood and so allow us to avoid some of the worst pitfalls associated with it.

The important part played by reflective practice in improving the social work task is the cen-tral theme of this book and has already been dealt with extensively, whilst this chapter is one of those charged with developing this theme into various practice areas. In it I suggest some ways whereby practioners might reflect upon the idea of 'professional dangerous-ness' as a way of improving practice. The first part is quite brief and only covers and sometimes extends those parts of reflective practice that appear relevant to this undertak-ing. The main part of the chapter explains and explores the concept of professional dangerousness and relates this to the practice of reflection within the social work task.

Reflective practice

In the introductory chapter we looked at how we might improve our professional practice in terms of Schön's reflection-on-action and reflection-in-action. The first involved us in thinking back on something already done, away from the action itself. The second, reflection-in-action, referred to thinking about what you are doing whilst you are doing it. As Schön himself says, phrases like thinking on your feet, keeping your wits about you, and learning by doing suggest not only that we can think about doing but that we can think about doing something while doing it (1991, p54). Thompson (2005) has recommended that we add a third concept here and reflect on our practice before, during and after the event. How then do these three concepts, reflection-before-action, reflection-in-action and reflection-on-action, relate to social work practice? Reflective practice is a dynamic concept and I think that the doing of 'good' social work has to mean that the social worker is continuously engaged in a process of reflective activity that includes all three of these elements. For us, reflection-before-practice involves us in gathering together and appraising what information is available both at the start of a case and throughout all of our involvement with the service user. Reflecting-in-action means always keeping the situation under constant review and revising or modifying our strategy as a result of these reflections. Reflecting-on-action allows us to learn from the experience so that we can benefit from any insights and use these to inform our future practice.

This need for continuous reflecting on practice can perhaps best be shown if we look very briefly at some of the dynamics operating within the Victoria Climbié case (Laming, 2003). Here, for example, a file had initially been opened on the case as economic migrants, so those involved would be viewing it in the context of the department's rules and policies for this group of people – concerning issues of homelessness and immigration which resulted in an offer of help to return to France. At this early stage 'reflection-before-action' on the part of the social worker allocated the case and others involved would have been around these policies. As the case progressed (reflection-in-action) and additional information started arriving – for example, one worker's description of the child as looking like an Oxfam poster – this may have helped to trigger the workers into seeing this as a child-protection case which required a conference had they reflected on the situation. By continuously reflecting-on-action the social worker may also have been able to recognise how her own and others' reactions to dealing with the case – feelings of distaste and intimidation when confronting the carers, the problem of language, the failure to acknowledge the 'stage-managed' visits – were all deflecting from the real need to protect Victoria from danger. Had this case been one where the social worker involved and those supervising her had been able to reflect on their practice in these ways it might have led to an important change of direction.

Crucially, the process of reflection must also include an appraisal of whatever relevant research evidence is available as well as ongoing references to colleagues'/supervisors' experiences as a guide to practice. I conducted a two-year project aimed at improving social work practice which involved giving child care social work teams the opportunity to discuss and reflect on their current cases through applying relevant and up-to-date research to their practice. This was mainly done by way of finding, accessing, reading and critically appraising likely relevant journal articles and applying them to their cases. An unintended, but beneficial consequence of the project was that the process allowed the social workers time to reflect on their 'live' cases (Wallis, 2004). In short, as was concluded in Chapter 1, it emphasised that 'Social workers need to be informed reflective practitioners'.

CASE STUDY

An example of reflection-on-action is given in the following extract, taken from a post-qualified social worker's notes reflecting on a recent child protection case.

Although I met with JoJo regularly to try to ascertain her views, looking back I think that if I had undertaken more structured sessions with her, for example individual work, I would possibly have gained more insight. I have to challenge myself and ask why I chose not to do this: is it because of restrictions of time, is it because I lack experience and confidence in this area or is it because of knowing that JoJo's mother may not be happy with this way of assessing? I think it is probably a combination of all three.

The time element is a real factor working with busy caseloads, however (if) it produces better outcomes in the long run, then I feel it is beneficial and worth putting in the time.

I lack experience, which affects my confidence. However I recognise that the only way I am going to develop in this area and gain confidence is to practise.

As for the third reason I have to remember that although I am trying to build up a working relationship with Mum, I am first and foremost JoJo's social worker and she is the priority.

ACTIVITY 6.1

After you have read the above reflections make a note of your answers to the following questions:

- *The social worker has developed the habit of being quite critical of his/her own behaviour, in this case where s/he was asked to contribute an assessment. Why do you think this may be an important skill?*

- *Why does s/he feel s/he should have 'undertaken more structured sessions' with JoJo?*

- *What are the three reasons given for not doing this?*

Comment

Now think about your answers. This social worker has developed the habit of reflecting on her practice to look for clues about what is happening in the child's family. In terms of assessing the relationships within the family, why is the failure of the social worker to work with JoJo on her own likely to be dangerous for JoJo?

You might also consider why it could have been dangerous for the social worker to have worked with JoJo on her own.

Do you think that this practitioner will now improve his/her practice as a result of this reflective activity?

So what is 'professional dangerousness'?

Professional dangerousness can occur when workers responsible for child protection leave a child at risk of significant harm as a consequence of their assumptions, attitudes or behaviour.

It is:

> *the process by which individual workers or multi-disciplinary networks can, mostly unwittingly, act in such a way as to collude with, maintain or increase the dangerous dynamics of the family.*

> (Reder and Duncan, 1999)

The above definition points to twin aspects of 'professional dangerousness'. The first is the process by which 'individual workers' can act in so-called dangerous ways. This aspect I will call 'dangerous behaviour'. The second aspect, where the contribution to dangerousness is by 'multi-disciplinary networks', I will call 'organisational dangerousness'.

Dangerous behaviour

In child care, professional dangerousness can occur when workers responsible for child protection leave a child at risk of significant harm as a consequence of their assumptions, attitudes or behaviour. Those involved frequently experience feelings of acute danger when facing hostile families, and can react irrationally to it. Aggressive or hostile behaviour towards social workers is like the elephant in the room that although all know it is there it is rarely addressed, and there are very real problems arising from practitioners not feeling able to reflect upon and discuss their fears and uncomfortable feelings about such experiences. Some commentators have described these feelings. One remarks on the:

> *infantile anxieties, which the task of child protection evokes in staff. Feelings of helplessness, of dependence and deference to authorities, of not knowing enough, of sticking to rules like a terrorised child, of fear and wanting to return to the normal world as soon as possible.*

> (Rustin, 2005)

Another has described his feelings when reacting to the danger in his early days as a social worker:

> *That sense in which you are so preoccupied with your own safety and survival that the safety and survival of the child becomes an afterthought, where just getting out of the house alive or relatively unscathed becomes the defining criteria of a good intervention – but of course this is never made explicit. Or when not seeing the child becomes not a source of concern, but a relief – in fact you have written to the family to pre-announce your visit not as a strategy to ensure they are there, but (un)consciously to sabotage the visit by giving them a chance to be out, or hiding in the house when you call. And when you knock and there's no reply, you skip back up the path and suddenly the world seems like a better place again, all because you don't have to struggle through another tortuous session with angry parents or carers.*

> (Ferguson, 2005)

Most families signal their distress that they are on the brink of a dangerous crisis in advance, if only what is being communicated can be understood. It takes professional skill to recognise the clues that are being given out in such cases and this skill needs careful development if it is to flourish and be sustained. We can miss even fairly basic clues if we don't reflect carefully on our practice. One 'paper' example of how, without careful reflection, simple clues can be missed in what was a relatively straightforward case, comes from a social worker's case study report. Here the writer evinced 'surprise' when a parent withdrew from a care plan of rehabilitation. This reaction came about even though the social worker's own earlier case notes clearly showed the parent's increasing lack of motivation and focus with the plan – important clues signalling the upcoming withdrawal. Social workers visiting a family in a potentially fraught child-abuse case where the carers are hostile and aggressive can react in many of the irrational ways described above. In so reacting they miss the clues and are unable (or unwilling) to decode the meaning of what is being communicated and thus cannot remain focused on the child's situation.

Social workers and students on placement have a responsibility to keep safe that entails a knowledge of self and an awareness and sensitivity to recognise situations where you or others may be intimidated or hurt. If you miss the clues you may well inflame an already hostile situation and escalate the aggression, resulting in you or a service user being harmed.

What counts as threatening behaviour?

We have all encountered threatening behaviour at some time or other – some more than others. According to one commentator, hostile and aggressive acts include the following: *shouting; swearing; using abusive language; taking up an aggressive stance, e.g. jabbing a finger in the face; making verbal threats in person or in writing; spitting; invasion of personal space; unwanted touching; throwing objects; brandishing a weapon; hitting; other physical or sexual attacks; preventing someone from leaving; damaging property* (Koprowska, 2005).

ACTIVITY 6.2

Look at Koprowska's above list of hostile and aggressive acts and:

- *make a note of those acts that you have experienced that were directed at you;*

- *go through these acts indicating which acts you experienced most often – trying to remember how you reacted;*

- *also indicate which one of these acts (e.g. shouting) you found the most frightening and how you reacted in those situations.*

Now think again about the acts on Koprowska's list and this time:

- *make a second list of those acts that you have witnessed that were directed at someone else;*

- *which one of these have you witnessed most often and what was your reaction?*

- *which of these frightened you the most?*

Comment

Looking back on these experiences, do you think there were times when there were some clues about impending violent behaviour that you missed? Often, when we are really frightened by such irrational behaviour we tend to react irrationally to it. Did your most frightening experience occur when there was just you and the aggressor or was there a group? It seems that some of the most violent acts of aggression occur within groups when the perpetrator is 'egged on'. Was the act that occurred the most the same as the one that frightened you most? If we experience bad behaviour often enough we tend to accept it as normal. Looking at your second list, was the act that frightened you most the same as the one in your first list? How did you react to this situation? We quite naturally tend to feel less threatened and perhaps even slightly relieved when the hostile act is directed at someone else rather than at us.

If you compare your answers to Activity 6.2 to a colleague's answers, you may well find that their answers are different to yours. We each react differently because of the prior experiences that we bring to each encounter and also according to our particular feelings at the time. Those of us who experienced excessive bullying at school, for example, may well view physical attacks as the most frightening aspect of aggressive behaviour and it is these kinds of threats that generally evoke patterns of irrational behaviour on our part.

ACTIVITY **6.3**

Can you recall a recent situation when you felt intimidated by the likely aggressive or violent behaviour of someone or something? Think of those times at home or at school or at work when you felt physically threatened by someone else's behaviour. Perhaps this happened when you were travelling on public transport or when confronted with some-body who was drunk? A good example of this would be if as a car user you had experience of 'road rage'.

Write down your answers to the following questions:

1. *What was it about the behaviour that made you feel intimidated?*

2. *Did it tend to make you react aggressively?*

3. *Did this sort of situation happen quite often or was it unusual?*

4. *Was this a situation that surprised you or did you expect it to happen?*

5. *Were there any clues to warn you that this might happen?*

6. *What did you do about it?*

7. *Did anyone else intervene?*

8. *Did your/their reaction make the situation worse or better?*

9. *How can you avoid it happening again?*

10. *What lessons did you learn from the experience?*

Comment

Think about your answers – maybe there were some clues leading up to the altercation that you missed because you were too apprehensive? This can happen quite often in stressful situations. Did you feel unable to do anything or did you have a protective strategy to deal with it? Reacting aggressively when feeling intimidated is not unusual although it generally escalates the violence. If it is something that occurred often (repetitive) or something you expected to happen (predictable), then you might have come to accept the behaviour as quite normal and not been particularly worried by it. The situation would have got even more inflamed or else perhaps defused depending on your and other people's reactions. One way of avoiding it happening again is to make sure you avoid that person in the future or else put into practice some of the lessons you learned from the encounter.

Compare your answers with those of a colleague or fellow student. Do you both have similar answers or do you find you each have different coping strategies?

These understandings can all be applied to the concept of professional dangerousness as this relates to our practice. Reflecting-on-action in this way about what happened/happens in our encounters with service users helps us to be more aware that our protective intentions and actions can inadvertently contribute to extending dangerous behaviour in some families. As Howe has theorised:

> The defence mechanisms used by all of us at some time or other, have their origins in (these) early attempts to cope with anxiety, abandonment, loss, conflict and emotional pain. In essence, the defences we use involve either (i) keeping painful information out of consciousness (for example denial and avoidance mechanisms) or (ii) redefining or trying to control painful experiences (for example projecting one's anger on to others and blaming them). One way of coping with these conflicting feelings is simply to try and avoid the conflict. Parents who cannot visit their sick children in hospital or social workers who make excuses not to see difficult clients are practising avoidance.
>
> (Howe, 1995, p93)

We know too that our professional practices (and systems) can mirror the very family patterns which we hope to change so that we start to behave in the same way as the families we deal with by perhaps accepting their abusive behaviour as 'normal'. This mirroring can also be mimicked within the workplace by creating 'scapegoats' to excuse unacceptable practices. A colleague in another agency may be blamed for what he or she did or did not do, or a more junior colleague may be blamed for their lack of skill or expertise.

Whilst not wishing to be alarming, there is no getting away from the fact that social workers often encounter hostility and aggression in their dealings with service users. Aggression may be directed towards family members, other service users, social workers or other professionals. In the course of his reflections on the Victoria Climbié case, Ferguson (2005) notes that while stress and violence in social work have been the subjects of important commentary, the sheer scale of resistance and hostility that professionals have to bear, particularly in child protection, and its implications requires further recognition.

Ferguson and O'Reilly (2001) reported that their study of all child care referrals made to three social work teams over a three-month period, revealed high levels of resistance, intimidation and violence against social workers. In at least 34 per cent of all cases that the social workers worked with they defined the parents or carers as involuntary clients who did not want a service. A powerful theme to emerge was the level of workers' anxiety not only for children's safety, but for their own safety and well-being.

However, it is vital to remember that generally, encounters between social workers and service users are not characterised by hostility. Many service users in all fields engage with services on a voluntary basis and get on well with their workers. Nonetheless, high numbers of staff across the whole social care workforce have experienced some form of aggression from service users to the extent that *social care staff have the lead position in being the most abused profession as compared to any other comparable working group* (Braithwaite, 2001, p5).

Ways of dealing with such hostility and aggression centre on reflection-before-action whereby safety can be improved both for the social worker and the child by good planning and anticipation, as well as reflection-on-action where the learning of good interpersonal skills for recognising and dealing with aggression is paramount. In such situations, the confrontational aspect between social worker and carer can often severely limit the available strategies for changing behaviour through 'reflection-in-action' (thinking on your feet). Schön has acknowledged this likely limitation and notes that what he calls:

> the action present (the period of time in which we remain in the same situation) varies greatly from case to case and in many cases there is time to think what we are doing.

> (Schön, 1991, p278)

He concludes that: *Indeed, our conception of the art of practice ought to give a central place to the ways in which practitioners learn to create opportunities for reflection-in-action* (Schön, 1991, p279). As social work practitioners we always need to be on the lookout for strategies that allow us to reflect and review our practice in the light of new information.

Organisational dangerousness

From our original definition, 'organisational dangerousness' covers the processes by which organisations, albeit unwittingly, act in such a way as to collude with, maintain or increase the dangerous dynamics of the family. Often, this form of professional dangerousness goes unrecognised because it is embedded in the culture of the organisation. Ruch (2002) considers that the importance of the concept of reflective practice to social work is that it permits a holistic understanding of the knowledge-generation process and stresses the importance of attending to both rational and irrational responses to practice encounters. Interestingly, in giving an example of the difference between the two responses, she describes a situation of 'organisational dangerousness' in child care practice involving a family with a history of sexually abusive relationships, where the departmental 'rational' response to concerns was to repeatedly devise ever more complex written agreements as if these would safeguard the child concerned in what was becoming an increasingly 'irrational' situation.

87

A further example is where a charitable organisation is blinded to racism by its own culture and is described in a book by Gould and his colleagues. Here, a voluntary agency working in the homeless sector was unable to recognise that it was the agency's white, middle-class, female culture that made it unable to appreciate the problems with clients that their black reception staff faced (Gould and Baldwin, 2004, p146).

Yet other instances of organisational dangerousness occur when a bureaucratic procedural response to a perceived problem can actually make a situation worse. There are other ways by which an institutional culture can work against good practice, particularly when, as now, social work departmental guidelines are dictated by resources. This can mean that social workers lose focus and apply the perceived needs of the service user to the eligibility criteria instead of what may be required in the care plan. This typically draws a response of *Well, we know there's no money in the kitty* and points to a culture of inevitability and belief that this is just part of the job that is present in many social service agencies.

CASE STUDY

Eight-year-old Victoria Climbié died in February 2000 from hypothermia, malnutrition and physical abuse suffered at the hands of her carers, a great-aunt and her cohabitee. The great-aunt brought Victoria from the Ivory Coast to France and then to London, supposedly to improve her education. During the last ten months of her life, Victoria had been known to the social services departments of four local authorities and two police child-protection teams and admitted with suspected non-accidental injuries to the paediatric wards of two different hospitals in the space of ten days.

The Climbié Report (Laming, 2003) notes that on many occasions although various professionals from all disciplines had information concerning Victoria's plight they did not act on it. Many reasons have been put forward to explain why what was seen to be an overworked and undersupported workforce failed to act. But it has also been suggested that this kind of paralysis was due to the underlying psychological and emotional dynamics of the impact of having to work with violent clients (Ferguson, 2005). In relation to social work practice, we can see this failure to act in the way that many of the proposed visits to the family by social services and the police did not take place. The report describes Kouao and Manning (the carers) as being routinely aggressive and menacing and also how they were able to stage-manage the pre-announced visits to the flat. The combined effect was that although by this time agencies were concerned enough to consider a visit, Victoria was never interviewed. There were in addition communication/language problems that were never resolved – the family spoke French.

The professional dangerousness exhibited here was at two levels. First, as in this case, all of those involved in such situations feel intimidated by the aggressive behaviour of the carers and sought to avoid contact with the family because of this. Secondly, this avoidance strategy is compounded by an element of distaste and fear brought about by the condition of the family. Victoria was diagnosed early on in the case as having scabies – and two social workers and a police officer gave the fear of getting infected as their reason for not visiting the home.

ACTIVITY 6.4

Re-read the above case study about the Victoria Climbié case and make a note of your reaction to it. Perhaps you can discuss with a colleague or fellow student what you both feel and whether you both have the same feelings and emotions about the case.

Now note down your answers to the following questions.

- *In the last ten months of Victoria's life the family was always on the move. How did this contribute to the organisational dangerousness exhibited in this case?*

- *What were your feelings after reflecting on this case? No doubt, even at this remove, we all feel a sense of shock and horror at what happened to Victoria. Yet our feelings would not be as intense as for those individuals (doctors, nurses, social workers) who witnessed her predicament at first hand and yet failed to act. Why do you think they never acted?*

- *On reflection, how might the effects of this aspect of professional dangerousness be lessened in the future?*

- *A key part of the professional dangerousness in this case was the failure of social workers to visit the family and to communicate with Victoria on her own. One reason for this may have been their reluctance to visit the family due to feelings of intimidation and also distaste for the conditions. On reflection, what strategies do you think they or their employers could have adopted so as to minimise this danger?*

- *What lessons were you able to learn from reflecting on this case and how could you incorporate them into your future practice? Compare your answers with those of your colleague or fellow student. Did you both have similar answers?*

Comment

This was a clear instance of 'professional dangerousness' both on the part of those professionals who were directly charged with protecting Victoria and the organisations within which they worked and should help us to appreciate the importance of reflecting on its effects in our own practice to avoid anything similar happening again.

C H A P T E R   S U M M A R Y

In conclusion I want to draw together some of the main practical suggestions that will assist you in trying to avoid the effects of professional dangerousness when you reflect on your practice.

- When reflecting-before-action – before every visit to a family you should find out as much as you can by reviewing the case notes and discussions with colleagues. When planning for your encounter you should track down any related research tied to the reason for your visit to help you to plan your strategy. Be aware of the way your own reaction to any hostile behaviour can prevent you from carrying out a proper assessment of the situation within the family.

- When reflecting-in-action – whilst interviewing a family with regard to child protection try not to mirror any observed aggressive behaviour in your dealings with the carers and set out the non-negotiable areas (such as seeing the child on its own) at an early stage in the relationship.

- Always set aside some time for reflecting-on-action – reviewing features of the case after the visit, to allow you to learn future strategies that will allow you to avoid, or at least minimise, the effects of the problems associated with professional dangerousness. This could include a change in direction of your intervention, such as in the Climbié case, to alter it from child in need to child protection.

- Finally, think 'outside of the box' so you can see in what ways the culture of the organisation you work within may work so as to enhance professional dangerousness rather than inhibit it and try to compensate for this in dealing with your cases.

FURTHER READING

Braithwaite, R (2001) *Managing aggression*. London: Routledge.
This is a useful guide to strategies for managing aggression.

Koprowska, J (2010) *Communication and interpersonal skills in social work*. 3rd edition. Exeter: Learning Matters.
Chapter 9 of this book will help you to recognise some of the clues that point to likely aggressive behaviour.

Chapter 7

Gender and reflective practice

Chris Smethurst

ACHIEVING A SOCIAL WORK DEGREE

This chapter will enable you to meet the following National Occupational Standards for Social Work:

Key Role 2: Plan, carry out, review and evaluate social work practice, with individuals, families, carers, groups, communities and other professionals
- Interact with individuals, families, carers, groups and communities to achieve change and development and to improve life opportunities.

Key Role 4: Manage risk to individuals, families, carers, groups, communities, self and colleagues
- Assess, minimise and manage risk to self and colleagues.

Key Role 5: Manage and be accountable, with supervision and support, for your own social work practice within your organisation
- Manage and be accountable for your own work.
- Work within multi-disciplinary and multi-organisational teams, networks and systems.

Key Role 6: Demonstrate professional competence in social work practice
- Work within agreed standards of social work practice and ensure own professional development.
- Manage complex ethical issues, dilemmas and conflicts.
- Contribute to the promotion of best social work practice.

It will also introduce you to the following academic standards as set out in the social work subject benchmark statement.

3.1.4 Social work theory: The relevance of psychological and physiological perspectives to understanding individual and social development and functioning

3.1.5 The nature of social work practice
- The nature and characteristics of skills associated with effective practice.
- The integration of theoretical perspectives and evidence from international research into the design and implementation of effective social work intervention.
- The process of reflection and evaluation, including familiarity with the range of approaches for evaluating welfare outcomes, and their significance for the development of practice and the practitioner.

3.2.5 Skills in personal and professional development
- Reflect on and modify your behaviour in the light of experience.
- Handle inter-personal and intra-personal conflict constructively.

Introduction

This chapter will ask you to reflect upon the impact of gender on your practice as a student, or qualified social worker. Specifically, it will help you to explore how your identity as a man or a woman may influence your behaviour and attitudes in practice. This chapter will also ask you to reflect on the extent to which your practice is influenced by others' expectations of what roles and behaviours are appropriate for you as a man or a woman. To get you started with this process, the following Activity 7.1 will ask you to reflect on your own experiences of being a male or female social work student or practitioner.

ACTIVITY 7.1

- *Does your identity as a man, or as a woman, bring you any advantages as a social worker?*

- *Are there any disadvantages?*

Comment

These questions are integral to any reflection you may undertake concerning the impact of your gender upon your practice. We will explore some of these themes in detail and so it may be useful to return to this exercise once you have read the chapter, as you may find that some of your answers to the questions may change in the light of what you are about to read. However, before we proceed, we need to acknowledge some of the difficulties that you may encounter when reflecting on gender.

Reflecting on the influence of gender in social work practice

As a social work student you will have encountered discussions of gender in relation to anti-oppressive practice. It is also likely that you will have been asked to reflect on the impact of gender in your relationships with service users, and with your colleagues and supervisors. However, when reflecting on the impact of gender in social work practice, students are confronted with a range of potentially conflicting perspectives. Some authors highlight the distinctive differences between male and female socialisation, and behaviour. Typically, these authors have highlighted the discrimination and oppression that women experience in male-dominated societies. In fact, it is argued that the study of gender has, until comparatively recently, focused primarily on women's experiences (Simpson, 2004).

Within social work, feminist perspectives have been particularly effective in ensuring that social workers are made aware of the discrimination and disadvantage that women encounter. Similarly, throughout their careers, it is also likely that social workers will encounter the consequences of abuse, violence and criminal activity: the overwhelming majority of this behaviour is perpetrated by men. Therefore, it is unsurprising that a considerable body of literature has explored the links between a range of social problems and the nature of 'masculinity'. In essence, this literature highlights the problems that men cause and asks whether there is something specifically problematic with male biology, psychology and socialisation.

However, other authors suggest that there is a greater degree of fluidity between men's and women's experiences and behaviour. Although these perspectives acknowledge the continuing oppression of women, and the problems caused by men, they reject the notion that men and women can be defined by fixed notions of masculinity and femininity. The range of perspectives concerning gender can be potentially very confusing for students, who may be looking for some certainty in their attempts to apply theory to their own experiences.

Arguably, our understanding of the process of reflection should help us with this confusion. The work of Schön (1983, 1991) suggests that we should be wary of attempting to uncritically apply particular theory, or rejecting it if it does not appear to correspond to our own experience. He asks us to engage in a 'reflective conversation' where we blend our theoretical knowledge with our own personal experience to gain a greater understanding of a specific situation. Schön allows for, and positively embraces, the notion that real life practice situations can be messy, involve uncertainty, and may challenge our preconceptions and beliefs.

It is clear that Schön's idea of a reflective practitioner requires honesty and openness on the part of the individual engaging in the 'reflective conversation'. I would suggest that this level of openness may occasionally be problematic if students are required to share their reflections with supervisors or fellow students. My experience as a social work educator suggests that gender is one of the issues where students may be anxious of 'saying the wrong thing', or using the 'wrong' language. For example, Gough (2001) highlights male students feeling the need to 'defend' their gender or 'bite their tongue'. Consequently, one could envisage students giving 'lip service' to particular language and behaviour, that they feel is expected of them, without really reflecting on their own attitudes and feelings. This last point suggests particular risks: Arshad (1996) coins the term the 'anti-sexist sexist' for those individuals who learn the language of gender equality, but do not see the need to reflect on their own attitudes and practice.

ACTIVITY 7.2

Reflect on your experience of how gender was addressed in your social work training:

- *Try and recall one specific session or topic; how did you feel during and after the session?*

- *In what ways did it inform your understanding of practice?*

- *Were there any aspects of this session that were unsuccessful? Why do you think it was unsuccessful?*

What do we mean when we talk about 'gender'?

'Gender' is often used interchangeably with 'sex' when referring to the distinction between men and women. However, 'sex' seems to imply distinctions based upon biological difference, whereas 'gender' can be understood more in terms of the individual's personal identity. This identity can incorporate physical characteristics, but may also be influenced by practices and expectations that are culturally determined. Consequently, individuals may learn to define themselves in relation to the characteristics and behaviours that are deemed to be 'typical' of men, or of women; 'masculine' and 'feminine' respectively. Sociologists and psychologists have been particularly interested in the ways through which individuals understand the 'gender rules' of masculinity and femininity. At one level this might seem obvious; you can probably immediately conjure up an image of a 'masculine' man or a 'feminine' woman. However, you might consider the extent to which your definitions are merely stereotypes.

ACTIVITY 7.3

From the following list of roles and characteristics, note down those you would classify as being associated with masculinity and those with femininity:

Physically strong, decisive, assertive, caring, loving, commanding, sensitive, aggressive, emotionally detached, nurturing, empathic, dynamic, rational, provider, breadwinner, home-maker, violent, dominant, competitive, sensual, risk-taker, stoic, tough, a people person, independent, entrepreneurial, a good listener, giving, values relationships, reflective, takes charge.

Comment

You may have found that it was relatively easy to clearly define some of the characteristics as being stereotypically masculine or feminine. However, some of the characteristics could perhaps apply to both genders, or increasingly be seen as not gender specific. This is not surprising if we accept that masculine and feminine roles and behaviour are less clearly defined than they might have been in the past, and are not merely determined by biological difference.

CASE STUDY

Lynn is in her late forties and has embarked on social work training, having spent the last 15 years raising a family. She is now in her second year at university and has been pleasantly surprised how well she has done academically. Reflecting on her own experiences of school, she realises that she was not encouraged to fulfil her potential. Although her brother was encouraged to go to university, Lynn's parents believed that girls should not be encouraged to pursue academic or professional careers. Lynn married young, but is now divorced; reflecting back, she realises that her ex-husband always seemed to be threatened by her intelligence and was absolutely set against her going to college.

Through talking to other women on the course Lynn has noted that hers was not a unique experience.

Lynn has found that the teaching of gender issues on her course has helped her make sense of some of her experiences. Lynn was particularly interested to learn of the feminist perspectives on caring. She noted that, when her mother became ill, the family and other professionals seemed to expect Lynn to care for her; the same expectation did not seem to apply to Lynn's brother. Lynn remembers the stress and the guilt that she experienced trying to reconcile all the conflicting demands that were placed upon her.

MacInnes (1998) argues that, although the continuing oppression of women is evident in many areas of economic and social life, the historic demarcation between men's and women's social roles, behaviours and activities has become increasingly blurred.

It is argued that collective identities, such as class and gender, are giving way to forms of identity that are far more personalised (Kumar, 1995). Our aspirations play a big part in defining our personalised identity: that is, how we would like to see ourselves and how we would like others to see us. It has been suggested that personal identities can be thought of as being like: *designer lifestyles – chosen by the wearer rather than imposed by the sociologist or policy planner* (Carter, 1998, p8).

I find the comparison of personal identity with something you wear quite an interesting one: the things we wear make us feel good; they say something about the person we are and how we would like to be perceived. However, we need to exercise a degree of caution when assessing the extent to which our personal identities are a matter of choice: although there may be a blurring of boundaries between men's and women's roles, behaviour and aspirations; this is not the same as saying that differences do not exist. There is evidence that socialisation, and the pressure to conform to particular roles and behaviours that we perceive are *expected* of men and women, are still powerful in defining how we feel we *ought* to be. How we think others perceive us, and even *judge* us, are perhaps important considerations in understanding how we learn the gender rules of behaviour.

An example of the pressures to conform to a particular notion of femininity has been highlighted by a number of feminist authors: they have argued that there is a societal expectation that women will care for others; this involves both physical labour and emotional investment (Graham, 1983). These external expectations derive from women's biological identities as mothers, but also from a social construction of femininity that values women who are nurturing, caring and self-sacrificing. These images provide a powerful message to women about what is 'appropriately' feminine behaviour. For example, Miller (1986) argues that many women assess themselves through their ability to 'give' in relationships with others. These expectations are key features of female socialisation: arguably, women may not be consciously aware of them. Although many women are unwilling, or unable, to conform to society's expectation: in doing so, they risk being labelled as 'unfeminine' by others (Dalley, 1996). However, they may also view themselves as being deficient: female carers interviewed by Hicks (1988) expressed feelings of inadequacy, resentment and depression at their inability to meet their expectations of themselves, and the demands of others.

Men also have particular templates of what a man should be. Defining characteristics of masculinity have been identified by Bowl (1985, 2001) and can be summarised as: being successful in the role of breadwinner, provider and father; appearing to be strong, competent, decisive, assertive and independent; maintaining control of one's emotions to maintain the impression of being logical and rational.

Connell (2000) acknowledges that, of course, not all men conform to a particular image of the idealised man, nor do all men wish to define themselves according to a fixed notion of what a man should aspire to be. However, Connell coined the term *hegemonic masculinity*, which recognises that, although there may be many different ways of defining and being masculine, a dominant image of masculinity still exists which provides a template of how men are expected to be, or should aspire to be. Therefore, physical strength, heterosexuality, independence and the suppression of emotion and vulnerability are still presented in popular culture as idealised and valued masculine traits; against these, men can be compared and found wanting. Gay men, men who are nurturing and emotionally sensitive, men who do not conform to the idealised form of masculinity can still be masculine; but, they are at risk of being labelled as not being 'real men'. Similarly, hegemonic masculinity recognises that gender identity is not divorced from the issue of social power: hegemonic masculinity dominates all constructions of femininity and *subordinate masculinities*.

Although we have provided a very brief summary of a number of perspectives on gender, hopefully you will have gained an appreciation of the complexity of the issues. We can now begin to apply some of the perspectives we have discussed to our understanding of social work practice. In her chapter on emotional intelligence, Gill Butler argues that through *reflection-in-action* the emotionally intelligent practitioner understands what others expect from them, and how to behave or react 'appropriately' in a given situation. In relation to gender, I find it interesting to understand how practitioners learn to react appropriately, and the relationship between personal choice and how individuals feel that they *ought* to behave: specifically, what are the benefits of conforming to how we feel we ought to behave and what are the costs if we do not?

ACTIVITY 7.4

- *Make a list of the roles, behaviours and characteristics that you feel that you are expected to adopt as a social worker because you are a man or a woman.*
- *Which ones do you strongly identify with?*
- *Are there some that you reject?*

Gender roles in social work practice

Hood, *et al*. (1998) illustrate the extent to which women were perceived to bring to post-war British social work special qualities that were also seen as being essentially feminine: the ability to engage with others and *to set both children and adults at their ease* (Curtis Report 1946: para.446). Empathy, sensitivity and the ability to read and manage others' emotions are skills and qualities typically associated with women. Hochschild (1983) argues that women's greater facility with emotion is a valued and essential characteristic of occupations where women predominate: in fact, it should be recognised as being *emotional labour*. Gorman and Postle (2003) suggest that emotional labour is integral to good social work practice but, because it is seen as something women do naturally, it is often unrecognised or undervalued by social work agencies. Instead, greater value is often afforded to processes and qualities that are perceived as essentially masculine: managerial skills, the ability to remain emotionally detached, or technical skills with IT or administrative systems.

Perry and Cree (2003) highlight the small numbers of men applying for social work training and a number of authors have speculated whether social work is an unusual, or *non-traditional* occupation for a man (Williams, 1995; Christie,1998). There is conflicting evidence as to whether male social workers are *different* to other men: they may be more emotionally nurturing, for example (Cree, 1996). Alternatively, it has been argued that men may be attracted to aspects of child protection and mental health that reaffirm masculine constructions of power and dominance, or afford greater professional status (Christie, 1998). Williams (1995) suggests that men in non-traditional occupations may be uncomfortable with female-dominated work cultures and poor professional status; these men may quickly ascend the *glass elevator* of promotion to higher status management positions.

CASE STUDY

Luke is a social worker in a local authority children and families team. He qualified two years ago and has worked in this team since qualifying. He is the only man in the team and, with the exception of his team manager and the senior practitioner, is the longest serving team member. Luke enjoys what he calls the 'buzz' that he gets from his work, but finds that he sometimes feels stressed and out of his depth. However, he is always reliable and never lets anyone down: he feels quite pleased that other members of the team respect him and ask his advice. Luke thinks that he frequently gets allocated to work with difficult service users, particularly men. His manager often asks him to accompany female workers on their visits to potentially aggressive clients. Luke thinks that he has learned a lot from watching how his female colleagues defuse certain situations, but he also thinks that they appreciate his support in a crisis. Luke hopes that he can act as a role model to young male service users, to show them that men can be caring and sensitive, but still be men.

ACTIVITY 7.5

* Looking at the case study, can you identify any risks for Luke?

Comment

The characteristics of stereotypical forms of masculinity might help us to understand some of Luke's experiences. For example, we could question how easy it would be for Luke to admit when he was feeling stressed or out of his depth; this could be particularly problematic, as Luke seems to value the status he receives from being seen as capable and reliable. This may, of course, pose some risks for Luke, and perhaps for service users and colleagues too. Other risks may be identified in the apparent expectation that Luke's gender equips him to deal with difficult or aggressive clients: perhaps Luke and his manager might reflect on what exactly Luke is expected to do and be in these situations. If Luke hopes to be a role model, perhaps he may also consider the possible contradictions in the roles he is expected to perform at work.

RESEARCH SUMMARY

Simpson (2004) explored the experiences of men in female-dominated occupations and her findings suggest the following:

- *Women may not receive the same career development opportunities as their male colleagues, who may be fast-tracked or groomed for promotion, or receive enhanced training.*

- *Men may receive special consideration from female colleagues: this can include the dubious benefits of being 'mothered', but may also include being treated more leniently by female managers.*

- *Men may experience the assumed authority effect: masculine status results in deference from colleagues and other professionals and an assumption of competence and expertise.*

- *The assumption of competence can place men in professional situations that their knowledge and experience does not equip them to deal with.*

This research provides a useful insight into the way men and women interact in organisations: it would seem that, even in occupations where their numbers dominate, women experience considerable disadvantage compared to their male colleagues. However, men in female-dominated occupations do experience some negatives: Hicks (2001) suggests that male social workers may indeed be perceived as 'nice' and 'caring' men, but they also risk being characterised as 'soft' or 'effeminate'. In addition, men in direct care work with children may be viewed with suspicion.

Women moving into the male-dominated world of management may also be viewed with suspicion and hostility. However this hostility may originate from their colleagues, both male and female. To adapt to the dominant organisational culture women may, through choice or necessity, adopt behaviours that are associated with masculinity: toughness and emotional detachment (Kerfoot, 2001). It is perhaps of particular concern that a number of studies have suggested that, in order to be seen as capable and suitable for promotion, women need to suppress emotional displays lest they be seen as a sign of weakness. For men, too, it would appear that being 'professional' is associated with the suppression and denial of emotion. We will explore the implications of this in the next section.

Gender and the emotional impact of social work

In her chapter Gill Butler highlights the need for practitioners to be able to reflect upon their own and others' emotions, and argues that 'emotional intelligence' is an integral part of effective social work practice. It is, therefore, surprising that emotion is not referred to in the social work Key Roles or in the standards for post-qualifying training. Not only does social work's person-centred value base draw heavily on notions of caring, nurturing and emotional support, but social workers often engage with particularly distressing and emotionally challenging situations. Research has revealed the incidence of anxiety, fear and emotional distress in social work practice; yet, recognition and support within agencies is variable (Smith, 2005). The failure to acknowledge the emotional aspects of the work is convincingly addressed by Ferguson (2005) and summarised in Sandra Wallis' chapter on professional dangerousness.

ACTIVITY **7.6**

Think of an experience at work or on placement that you found to be emotionally challenging.

- *What did you feel at the time?*

- *Did you get any support at work? Who from?*

Comment

Smith (2005) demonstrates that the support of colleagues, including the line manager, is important in helping social workers deal with the anxiety and distress that they may encounter through their job. Failure to acknowledge and address the emotional impact of work can result in emotional 'burn out' (Hochschild, 1983) or lead to dangerous practice (Ferguson, 2005).

The following research summary highlights students' experiences on a Canadian social work programme. Although it does not specifically address gender, it will be helpful for you to reflect on whether any of the themes that we have discussed in this chapter might be relevant in understanding the students' reported experiences.

RESEARCH SUMMARY

Barlow and Hall (2007) interviewed 70 Canadian social work students and practice teachers about their experiences of upsetting events in practice. The research highlighted five key themes.

- *Client circumstances had a significant emotional impact on students. They sometimes felt overwhelmed and vulnerable. However, practice teachers sometimes underestimated the emotional impact of practice situations upon students.*

(continued)

RESEARCH SUMMARY *continued*

- *Students often doubted their competence when faced with emotional distress; they sometimes felt 'out of their depth' and believed that more should be done to prepare them for this aspect of practice.*

- *Management of potentially violent situations caused some level of anxiety for students. Students sometimes felt at physical risk even though they had not been directly threatened. Students also reported being sexually harassed by clients.*

- *Unsupportive practice teachers considerably heightened students levels of emotional anxiety. Students valued the opportunity to discuss their feelings about practice. However, uncertainty about who to trust increased students' feelings of vulnerability.*

- *Students felt uneasy navigating office politics, particularly in 'cliquey' environments. Students could feel isolated, and fearful of breaking unspoken agency or office rules.*

CASE STUDY

Julie is a social work student on placement. She has been working with a 15-year-old young person called Dan, who has a history of offending behaviour. Teachers and other social workers perceive Dan as being rather uncommunicative and aggressive, and Julie acknowledges that Dan's behaviour has often left her feeling anxious, frustrated and irritated. However, she tries not to show this in her work with Dan. In supervision Julie has recognised that some of her irritation stems from feeling that she is 'not getting through to Dan'; because this makes Julie doubt her own competence, she feels angry towards Dan. Julie learned that Dan had been in a fight outside school, where he was attacked by a group of young people. The teacher who Julie spoke to suggested that Dan had been 'winding people up, like he usually does', but Dan would not say anything about what happened. Julie visited Dan; she asked him to describe what had occurred. Dan started to speak, then began to cry. Julie was a bit taken aback: because Dan had always seemed so combative Julie had not expected him to cry. Dan quickly got embarrassed and said he was 'OK' and didn't want to talk about it. Julie changed the subject, then immediately regretted doing so.

ACTIVITY 7.7

Try and put yourself in Julie's position: what would you do next?

Comment

The case study illustrates a familiar question for social workers: how to respond to someone who is distressed. In this situation, Dan appears to have become embarrassed about crying in front of Julie. You might consider whether Julie was right not to explore the cause of Dan's distress: if not what could she have done differently? You might also reflect on whether it would have been easier, or more difficult, for both participants if they were both female, or if either the social worker or service user had been female.

C H A P T E R   S U M M A R Y

- The influence of gender is a key feature of social work practice, yet the range of theory can be confusing for students looking to apply a particular perspective to their own experiences.

- The work of Schön provides a useful framework for acknowledging and understanding that reflective practice requires a flexible and critical approach to the application of theory to the 'messy' real world of practice.

- Nevertheless, students could be reluctant to openly engage with and discuss some of the issues concerning gender. This may be because the issues could be seen as being contentious and students are anxious about 'saying the wrong thing'.

- Exploring some of the theory and research concerning gender, and reflecting on your own experiences, views and behaviour will help you understand how your gender impacts upon your experience of practice.

- It is beneficial to consider the emotional impact of social work and reflect upon how your gender may affect your responses to particular situations, and the support you may receive from others.

FURTHER READING

Christie, A (ed) (2001) *Men in social work*. Basingstoke: Palgrave.
This book provides a thorough and accessible summary of relevant debates.

Smith, M (2005) *Surviving fears in health and social care: The terrors of night and the arrows of day*.
London: Jessica Kingsley Publishers.
This book is an essential text for those who wish to understand more about the role of emotion in social work practice.

Chapter 8

Reflective practice on placement

Carleton Edwards

ACHIEVING A SOCIAL WORK DEGREE

This chapter refers to the practice placement component of achieving a social work degree and the following Key Roles and units of the National Occupational Standards.

Key Role 6 Demonstrate professional competence in social work practice
Unit 19 Work within agreed standards of social work practice and ensure own professional development
19.1 Exercise and justify professional judgements
19.2 Use professional assertiveness to justify decisions and uphold professional social work practice, values and ethics
19.3 Work within the principles and values underpinning social work practice
19.4 **Critically reflect upon your own practice and performance using supervision and support systems**
19.5 Use supervision and support to take action to meet continuing professional development needs
Unit 20 Manage complex ethical issues, dilemmas and conflicts
20.1 Identify and assess issues, dilemmas and conflicts that might affect your practice
20.2 Devise strategies to deal with ethical issues, dilemmas and conflicts
20.3 **Reflect on outcomes**
The following academic standards for social work, as set out in the subject benchmarking statement, also apply.
3.1.5 The nature of social work practice
The process of reflection and evaluation, including familiarity with the range of approaches for evaluating welfare outcomes, and their significance for the development of practice and the practitioner
3.2 Subject skills and other skills
All social work honours graduates should have shown the ability to reflect on, and learn from the exercise of their skills. They should understand the significance of the concept of continuing professional development and lifelong learning and accept responsibility for their own continuing development
4.2 Reflection on performance
A process in which a student reflects on past experience, recent performance, and feedback, and applies this information to the process of integrating awareness (including awareness of the impact of self on others) and new understanding, leading to improved performance.

Introduction

The purpose of this chapter is to consider and explore the use of reflective practice while you are undertaking practice learning during study for a social work degree.

As the course progresses your skills and insights into the use and benefits of reflective practice will develop.

After qualification, as a social worker you will embark upon continual professional development and will be assessed in practice to gain a post-qualifying award. The content of this chapter could also be used to explore reflective practice in this arena as well.

Although this chapter is aimed primarily at students, it should also be of interest and use to practice assessors. Practice assessors will need to take account of their students' individual circumstances. It is helpful not to immediately question students about their abilities as reflective practitioners but to approach the topic more circumspectly. Practice assessors who have seen students become hesitant and apprehensive when asked to relate theory to practice in the placement context will understand the need for a considered and facilitative approach. Indeed, practice assessors must in turn reflect upon how they will work effectively with students in this regard. Practice assessors will, therefore, be mirroring the process that students will be asked to engage with.

Overview

It is not planned here to extensively repeat the theoretical material on reflective practice in the preceding chapters of this book, and especially Chapter 1, which reviews the subject. Rather, this chapter is intended to explore practical ways in which reflective practice can be used in the placement, as well as to stimulate thinking about methods of incorporating it more broadly into the practice curriculum. However, the theoretical frame of reference is referred to in summary here in its relationship to the placement context.

Reflection can be expressed as considering practice, before, during and after the event (Thompson, 2000). Payne, in Adams et al. (2002), also captures this well, as *Thinking issues through in all their complexity and acting towards clients and others in a considered, thoughtful manner is the common sense meaning of reflection* (p124).

Reflection before intervention could be viewed as planning or forethought. Schön (1983) then uses the terms 'reflection in action' and 'reflection on action'. The former takes place during the practice episode, and would not be able to be described by the practitioner beforehand. The latter implies an evaluation of practice, which could also be informed by service user and carer feedback. All of these approaches would hopefully lead to the consideration of different and possibly better methods of practice.

> *The reflective approach recognises that theory is often implicit in the way professionals act and may or may not be congruent with the theory they believe themselves to be acting upon. This type of theory, or perhaps 'practice wisdom', is developed directly from practice experience – a 'bottom-up' type of process.*
>
> (Fook, 2002, p39)

This clearly implies that reflection is inductive rather than deductive. It also acknowledges that social work can be an intuitive craft, perhaps an art rather than, or as well as, a science. There is no mutual exclusivity between reflective practice and evidence and research-informed practice. There is also an implied recognition that knowledge and skills might need to be recreated by the social worker in response to changing and unpredictable practice situations. This idea resonates well with the current world of social work.

The key concepts therefore are that reflective practice on placement is a critical and analytic tool. It can be used in helping to integrate theoretical learning, gain insight, transfer knowledge and promote learning in depth. All of this has the ultimate aim of developing professional practice with the benefit of improved work with service users and carers.

National Occupational Standards

Assessment in practice comprises half of the qualifying training programme on both undergraduate and masters social work degrees. The Department of Health (DoH) gave a clear signal of the importance of assessment in practice when the new BA in Social Work was established by increasing the number of placement days from a minimum of 130 on the Diploma in Social Work to a minimum of 200 for the BA and Masters in Social Work. The DoH (2002) expressed some clear expectations about the importance of practice learning:

> *Practice is central to the new degree, with academic learning supporting practice, rather than the other way round.* (p1)
>
> *Ensure that the teaching of theoretical knowledge, skills and values is based on their application in practice.* (p3)

There are six key roles within the National Occupational Standards for social work. Key Role 6, Units 19 and 20, make a specific reference to your ability to reflect in practice.

You are practice-assessed against these National Occupational Standards criteria by your practice assessors, and must pass all of the units to proceed and qualify.

There is the usual difficulty of attempting to assess skills and ability within a competence assessment framework, sometimes referred to as a 'tick box' exercise. It can be relatively easy to discover whether you understand a certain sort of knowledge, such as legislation, policy and procedure. It is less easy to make a judgement about the ability to reflect on practice.

Units 19 and 20 referred to above occur at the end of the National Occupational Standards. This brings with it an implication that reflective practice is a skill that develops over the duration of social work training and with practice experience, but that it culminates at the summation of the course. It might be helpful to think of reflective practice developing over the duration of the qualifying course in stages:

1. *Awareness* of the concept;

2. *Understanding* of the concept;

3. An ability to take *action* as a result of understanding.

The taxonomy of learning in the cognitive domain is referred to in Chapter 1, with the development of learning from knowledge to understanding to application to analysis to synthesis to evaluation. This would fit with the model of learning moving from pedagogy to andragogy, with you finally taking responsibility for your own learning and becoming an autonomous worker, helping to create solutions to meet the individual needs of service users and carers. Assuming that we would all think about a practice intervention before the event, it could be considered that you are able to 'reflect on action' during the first practice placement. You can then progress to being able to 'reflect in action' as you are able to articulate connections between experience, feelings and theory (Watson and West, 2006) during practice on the second placement.

The ability to reflect on practice can then be transferred to continuous professional development and post-qualifying training. Newly qualified social workers are assessed on their ability to consolidate practice against the same National Occupational Standards in the first part of the post-qualifying awards.

On placement

To assist you to develop your thinking about reflective practice, it can be helpful to use a simile or metaphor as a tool. One effective simile is to consider a mirror as a reflecting surface. This is referred to in Chapter 1, whereby a mirror can reflect back to us what is going on in difficult situations. However, it is possible to extend the simile to incorporate an anti-oppressive practice perspective with the mirror not just reflecting an image straight back to you. If the mirror is at an angle it is possible to see things from a different perspective. Such a technique can be used as an attempt to explore and gain insight into the service users' and carers' points of view. This can consequently aid challenging assumptions and preconceptions as well as generally contributing to anti-oppressive practice. Any tool that enables insight into the service users' and carers' perspectives in general should help to facilitate an understanding of various ways of improving service delivery.

You might be relieved when you go on placement and are able to start doing 'real' social work. The immediacy of involvement with direct practice can mean that you neglect considering the influence of theory. Reflective practice can be the bridge from this lack of engagement with theory to a balanced or middle position that is a type of informed practice wisdom. Schön (1983) invites maintaining this position between the messiness of the 'swampy lowlands' of practice and the high ground of theory. This implies that social work is not a technical science but rather a craft that has a place for practice competence, wisdom and intuition. There is also the considerable benefit of processing learning from experience. An example of 'technical rationality' could be the strict application of eligibility criteria to an assessment of need or the medical model of treating mental illness without reference to the social context of the service user and carer. Reflective practice can facilitate the professional artistry of social work to take place, whereby holistic assessments are made, informed by the context of the episode and the service users' and carers' perspectives. Social workers tend to relate to this process as it can also be used in their professional context of perennial change, continually redefined networks, uncertainty and differing expectations. This would also relate to local authority social services' reorganisation, taking into account the disaggregation of adults' services and children and young people's services and the reconfiguration of services resulting from recent government initiatives such as *Every Child Matters* (DoH, 2004) and *Our health, our care, our say* (DoH, 2006).

The use of reflection by you in practice placements should ensure that your current and future practice is as good as possible. It will also maintain your professional development and therefore must also be of ultimate benefit to service users and carers.

Supervision

Reflection can be considered as an aid to learning, and as a way of integrating theory and practice by recognising the dynamic interface between the two. This can be most effective for you when issues are brought to supervision with the practice assessor. The supervisory relationship also ameliorates the risk of your reflection occurring in an uncritical vacuum

The practice assessor and you are in a special learning relationship. Within agencies, the supervision of staff is often based on worker accountability to the agency and its policies. Although these conditions also apply to the qualifying student, there is a greater commitment to, and time spent on, developing your knowledge, skills and values. However, in the final analysis, all of these endeavours within supervision aspire to improve practice with a benefit for service users and carers. It is important for the practice assessor and you to agree a common understanding of reflective practice.

The practice assessor and you can utilise a range of tools to assist reflection on practice, such as the use of a reflective journal and critical incident analysis.

Parker (2004) describes the benefits of keeping a reflective diary or learning log based on your experience with a *focus on actual events or situations that you have experienced during one's practice learning* (p32). This should not just be a descriptive account, but incorporate reactions, thoughts, theories, learning and hoped-for outcomes. Cottrell (2003) identifies that such a diary can have two main benefits (p67):

The act of writing things down helps you to clarify your thoughts and emotions, to work out strategies, and to focus on your own developments and progress. A written record will help you see how you are progressing from week to week and from term to term.

ACTIVITY 8.1

Both the practice assessor and you:

- *record your definitions of reflective practice;*
- *compare definitions;*
- *agree a common understanding of reflective practice;*
- *agree when and how to make use of reflective practice;*
- *discuss regularly in supervision.*

ACTIVITY 8.1 continued

Within supervision there can be a discussion of reflection in practice about a difficult situation recently experienced, and you should be able to respond to the following questions.

- *What was the event? Who was involved? Was it planned/unplanned?*
- *How did you act/respond?*
- *How did you feel?*
- *What skills did you use?*
- *What theories can be applied to this event?*
- *Did you work in an anti-oppressive way?*
- *Were there any issues now apparent that you were not aware of at the time?*
- *What did you learn from the event and this discussion?*
- *How can you relate this to future practice?*

Comment

This latter questioning exercise could be performed on a regular basis within supervision, and even be a standing item on the agenda. It would be interesting for both the practice assessor and you to note any progress over time, which might be evidence of developing competence. For example, an ability to apply theory, consider anti-oppressive strategies or even reflect might increase over the duration of the placement.

The practice assessor and you have an array of other tools at your disposal to promote reflective practice. A critical incident analysis is an individual account of an episode of practice that is explored in some depth. You could describe a practice episode and your intervention and the outcome in supervision, incorporating critical analysis and reflection. The practice episode could be of a few minutes' duration or a whole interview or intervention. An expanded critical incident analysis could develop into a process recording, which would use the extended recording of an intervention to promote critical analysis and reflection. Again, this can be used in the supervision session with the practice assessor. Critical incident analysis can also be a good exercise for you to do in a group, guided by a practice assessor in a mentor role.

The practice assignments on the BASW at the University of Chichester, completed when students are on placement, require them to comment on personal reflection. These are marked by the practice assessor and contribute towards the overall assessment of the student's practice while on placement. An example of one such assignment follows, and could be used as a piece of written work completed by you and submitted to the practice assessor. It is an assignment of 2,500 words with references. The aim is to demonstrate problem-solving skills and critical analysis of an assessment of risk, using an example from your practice with a service user, family and/or carers involved in their care. In writing the assignment the student must:

- carry out a comprehensive assessment with an individual, a family, or a carer, where there are issues of risk to an individual or others in the family, group or community;

- describe how the assessment was carried out and any outcomes;

- demonstrate partnership with those in the assessment process;

- critically analyse dilemmas involved in assessing risk and promoting choice;

- identify theories used to underpin the assessment and the outcome;

- show personal reflection on what they might have done differently and identify future learning needs.

Key Roles 2 and 4 of the National Occupational Standards could be evidenced by your practice referred to in the assignment.

Key Role 2 Plan, carry out, review and evaluate social work practice, with individuals, families, carers, groups, communities and other professionals

Unit 9 Address behaviour, which presents a risk to individuals, families, carers groups and communities

9.1 Take immediate action to deal with behaviour which presents a risk

9.2 Work with individuals, families, carers, groups and communities and others to identify and evaluate situations and circumstances that may trigger the behaviour

9.3 Work with individuals, etc., on strategies and support that could positively change the behaviour

Key Role 4 Manage risk to individuals, families, carers, groups, communities, self and colleagues

Unit 12 Assess and manage risks to individuals, families, carers, groups and communities

12.1 Identify and assess the nature of risk

12.2 Balance the rights and responsibilities of individuals, families, carers, groups and communities with associated risk

12.3 Regularly monitor, re-assess and manage risk to individuals, families, carers, groups and communities

---

This assignment could be graded as a pass or fail by the practice assessor, and discussed in supervision. It would be significant if a student did not pass the assignment and a resubmission could be required. Another failed attempt could question their readiness to proceed and pass the placement. Practice assignments can serve a similar function to report writing in that they are a good test of formal presentation, use of English, ability to present ideas clearly, etc. My experience is that writing such practice assignments is valued, even enjoyed, by most students and a popular learning tool. They can also provide good evidence for the National Occupational Standards.

Some students can become hesitant when directly asked to reflect on practice. However, your practice assessor can encourage you to reflect by asking you to consider your practice before and after an intervention during supervision sessions either side of the practice episode. This is explored in the following section.

Case studies

Observations of practice are crucial to the task of your practice assessment, and a most productive source of evidence of competence. They also provide an excellent way to enable you to reflect on practice by having a structured discussion during a briefing session just prior to the observation and a discussion and feedback session afterwards. Service user and carer feedback is valuable and can also inform this process, especially after the event. Attention should be paid to ensuring that relevant service user and carer feedback is gathered appropriately and that the process is not tokenistic (Edwards, 2003; Parker, 2004).

Consider the following case studies. Please put aside, for the purpose of the exercise, that the case studies are from different settings in both adults' services and children and young people's services, and whether they are typical or credible.

CASE STUDY A

Part 1

You are a student placed in a family centre that predominantly works with families where there are concerns about parenting and/or child-protection issues. The centre tries to work in partnership with parents and have a policy of complete openness with service users and carers.

A social worker from the local office has referred a family and requested a parenting assessment. Claire is 16 and her partner Peter is 17. They both have mild learning difficulties and have a history of drinking and taking drugs. Peter is known to have a short temper with occasional aggressive outbursts. They have a son Jordan, who is 12 months old and slightly underweight. The parents do not seem to always maintain a focus on his needs, e.g. missing medical appointments. You are in the middle of your placement and will be doing a parenting assessment for the first time by yourself, but able to consult your practice assessor or other centre workers at any time. The health visitor has suggested a child protection investigation, but this is not thought appropriate at this stage, as the criteria have not been met.

CASE STUDY B

Part 1

You are a student in an adults' services fieldwork team, mainly working with older people in the community. A referral has been received about Harry and Mary, both in their 90s. They have a limited income and live in a dilapidated house. They have a son Gordon who lives nearby but rarely seems to visit. Harry is a large man and now with signs of memory loss. Mary is the carer and has a smaller build. She has limited mobility and is often unwell. A neighbour has reported that Gordon is not a nice person, and has been encouraging his parents to sell the house and go into a residential home. He has been heard shouting at them and calling them 'old fools who can't care for themselves any longer'. You are in the middle of your placement and will be doing an assessment for the first time by yourself of the couple's needs, but able to consult your practice assessor or other colleagues at any time.

ACTIVITY 8.2

Imagine that, as a student social worker, you have been allocated these two cases. Please pause here and:

- write down some of your initial thoughts and feelings on being allocated the cases;
- consider what information you think will influence your assessments.

You have now had the initial meetings with the service users in both cases.

CASE STUDY A

Part 2

You met Claire and Jordan to start the assessment. Claire seemed to be more articulate and insightful than you imagined. She described a past of drinking with friends, although she was more restrained when pregnant. She and Peter are occasional cannabis users, but ensure that they only use when Jordan is in bed and keep the drugs well out of his reach. Claire knows that she is a young mother, but said that she adores Jordan, and will only do what is in his best interests. You feel that she is sincere, and warm to her. In fact, she reminded you of a friend from your past. Claire was happy to fully co-operate with the assessment. She hopes to stay in her relationship with Peter, although they are under strain with little money and living in a B&B. Claire said that Peter had never been aggressive towards her or Jordan. Claire then commented that her health visitor seems to be overly critical of her, commenting on her young age as a mother. The introductory session was finishing when Peter came in to collect Claire and Jordan. He described feeling awkward in a centre where he is usually the only male present.

CASE STUDY B

Part 2

You visited Harry and Mary by appointment, and started an initial assessment. One of their first comments was how young you seem to them, and they asked you about your life and family. They, in turn, seemed kind and generous and reminded you of your own grandparents.

Harry was clearly suffering from memory loss, occasionally forgetting who you are. He then got upset when he became aware of his diminished abilities. Mary talked of her isolation and struggle to maintain herself and her husband, getting shopping, doing laundry, etc. She felt that she could not cope any longer like this, and although she would like to remain at home with her husband thought it might be better to go into a residential home and not cause any further bother to anyone. Mary commented that their son thought that residential care would be better for them. There are brochures about residential homes on the table, and Mary said that Gordon has had the house valued by an estate agent. You were about to leave, and when shaking hands, realised that Mary had bruises on her arms. You quickly asked about the bruises. Mary said that they were caused accidentally and that she bruises easily now that she is so old.

ACTIVITY **8.3**

As the student social worker working with both Case Studies A and B:

- *Were you developing your thinking as you were reading the second parts of the case studies (possible reflection in action)?*

- *Refer back to the notes you made in Exercise 8.2, and consider whether your thinking about the cases has significantly changed.*

- *On reflection, what are the most significant practice issues that you can identify in the case studies (reflection on action)?*

- *What are the rights and responsibilities of all of the people mentioned?*

- *Is there any overall learning that you can draw from considering both cases?*

Comment

This exercise can be helpful for both the practice assessor and you in gauging your ability to be able to be analytical, critical and, of course, reflective. The case studies provoke some good material for consideration and debate. To what extent can we empathise with Claire and Mary? Do we have prejudices against Peter and Gordon and, if so, on what are they based? What theories might apply to these cases? Does our thinking change over time as we gain and process more information?

This type of exercise could be done between the practice assessor and you in supervision. The format of the questions could also represent a model for the discussions that could take place based upon an observation of your practice by the practice assessor. There could be a discussion prior to and after your practice being observed by the practice assessor, incorporating references to reflection, any service user and/or carer feedback as well as feedback from the assessor observer. The benefits of the exercise are summarised by the following quote:

> While reflection is itself an experience it is not, of course, an end in itself. It has the objective of making us ready for new experience. The outcomes of reflection may include a new way of doing something, the clarification of an issue, the development of a skill or the resolution of a problem. A new cognitive map may emerge, or a new set of ideas may be identified.
>
> Boud et al. (1985, p340)

RESEARCH SUMMARY

The research available on reflection by social work students on practice placements is limited. A good starting point is a consideration of whether there is any consensus about what reflection is within social work education, and whether it should be taught and then assessed on social work courses (Ixer, 1999).

The current emphasis on research and evidence-based practice, as well as the assessment of competence, is prevalent within social work education. This could suggest that the good application of knowledge and skills is the main criterion for the practice assessment of social work students. However, reflection can enable students to gain important learning from practice experience. A qualitative study based on the reflective learning logs of social work students in Hong Kong demonstrated that disturbing events on placement were significant in promoting practice learning and progress. They were the main catalyst for the students' critical appraisal of practice and the development of improved professional responses Lam et al. (2007).

C H A P T E R   S U M M A R Y

This chapter has identified the importance of reflective practice for you in placement on a qualifying course. In summary, the main points are:

- read up on the subject;
- become familiar with reflection while on placement as a tool to improve practice;
- overcome any natural apprehension by putting reflective practice on the agenda for supervision and other discussions;
- note improvements in practice as a result of using reflection and celebrate these outcomes;
- carry the skill into post-qualifying practice and training – hopefully you will also become a practice assessor one day.

Practice assessors need to use their skills to develop your practice, and the processes and techniques identified here can assist in this. It is clear that reflection is a useful skill to develop and consolidate during professional training, and that it will then be available throughout the career of a social worker. The benefits appear to be for the individual student social worker, the placement, future employers and ultimately for service users and carers. Perhaps the most significant skill that reflective practice bestows is that it promotes professional autonomy. The hope is that you will then continue to use refection when qualified, and that it will enhance your continual professional development. Parker (2004) identifies the benefits of reflection in developing analysis and effectiveness in practice, and that it is a skill that is transferable and durable. In this light, social work practice clearly has a place for reflective practice both now and in the future.

Parker, J (2010) *Effective practice learning in social work*. 3rd edition. Exeter: Learning Matters.
This book provides a comprehensive exploration of the essential components of good practice learning, such as the integration of theory, reflection, assessment and the use of supervision. The author demonstrates a good knowledge of, and insight into, contemporary practice learning issues.

Watson, D and West, J (2006) *Social work process and practice*. Basingstoke: Palgrave.
This book provides a good exploration of the knowledge, skills and values that underpin and inform contemporary social work practice and processes. It includes a separate chapter on reflection and supervision.

Part Three

Maintaining reflective practice

Chapter 9
Working with your manager

Terry Scragg

A C H I E V I N G   A   S O C I A L   W O R K   D E G R E E

This chapter will help you to meet the following National Occupational Standards.
Key Role 5: Manage and be accountable, with supervision and support, for your own social work practice within your organisation
• Use professional and managerial supervision and support to improve your practice
Key Role 6: Demonstrate professional competence in social work practice
• Use professional and organisational supervision and support to research, critically analyse, and review knowledge based practice
• Critically reflect upon your own practice and performance using supervision and support systems
• Use supervision and support to take action to meet continuing professional development needs
It will also introduce you to the following academic standards as set out in the social work subject benchmark statements:
2. Defining principles
Acquire the habits of critical reflection, self-evaluation and consultation, and make appropriate use of research in the evaluation of practice outcomes
3.1.5 The nature of social work practice
The process of reflection and evaluation, including familiarity with a range of approaches for evaluating welfare outcomes and significance for the development of practice and the practitioner
3.2.5 Skills in personal and professional development
Take responsibility for your own further and continuing acquisition of knowledge and skills.

Introduction

In this chapter you will be introduced to the world of management, particularly the work of the first line manager, who is the person you will come into regular contact with both as a student and when newly appointed to a social work post. Working with your manager will be one of your most significant workplace relationships and it is important that you understand the changing world of social work management, the pressures and demands placed on first line managers and how you can work effectively with your manager. For the purposes of this chapter we have assumed that you are working with your manager in a practice supervision role.

The first part of the chapter will examine the role of the first line manager, who has key responsibilities in terms of leading a team, managing resources and allocating work, maintaining standards and supporting staff who are directly involved in providing or arranging services. The second part is concerned with how you can make best use of the skills of your manager and what you need to do to ensure that you are getting the best from your relationship with your manager. Here we are talking about 'managing your manager', in other words knowing what you have to do to ensure that you meet your manager's needs and at the same time receive the support you need to do your job effectively, develop your skills and advance your career. The third part focuses on the important work of supporting staff and those activities that enable staff to perform well, including supervision, consultation and review. All these activities have a valuable developmental function, particularly helping the newly qualified social work practitioner to develop a critical awareness of the potential of reflective learning.

Part one: the work of the first line manager

First line managers have to make best use of their staff and the other resources they control. They need a clear understanding of the task and how it can be achieved, an understanding of the skills and abilities of team members, and the agency's wider resources. They also need knowledge of how the staff team can mobilise resources in the community, either through partnership with other provider organisations, or by direct intervention. To achieve this they have to establish a form of work allocation and workload management that is achievable within the resources available to them to ensure staff can manage their personal workloads without creating stress and burnout (Rosen, 2000).

They also have a key role in supporting, monitoring and developing social care practice. They are the 'bridge' between senior management and frontline staff and service users, interpreting organisational policies and procedures, legislative requirements and practice standards to their teams. They also play an important role in communicating and explaining management decisions and in turn provide information where policies and procedures are not working, and represent the opinions of frontline staff to senior management. In the words of Rosen (2000), *their job is to hold together what can seem like different worlds.*

In their research on first line managers, Henderson and Seden (2003) argue that employers want managers to manage the dilemmas, constraints and challenges which face teams at the front line of services, where they operate in situations of conflicting requirements. From an analysis of managers' job descriptions, Henderson and Seden identified the requirements of employers falling into three main functions, which were in turn identified by first line managers who participated in their research. These are:

- **strategic** they are required to develop strategies, systems and procedures to meet the overall objectives of the service;
- **operational** they have to ensure that the service is effectively managed and that they adhere to departmental objectives and resolve operational problems;
- **professional** they have to take responsibility for managing all staff, including induction, supervision, training, development and appraisal. They need to ensure that staff

are empowered to undertake the tasks allocated to them, to consult them and involve them in decision-making. They also need to provide effective support and take corrective or disciplinary action where necessary.

What these three functions tell us is that first line managers face a number of dilemmas on a regular basis. They have to focus on the operational and professional components of their role – the day-to-day support and supervision of staff, allocating work, developing and enabling team members, and ensuring that they meet practice standards whilst at the same time responding to the demands of senior managers as part of the strategic planning process based on their local knowledge.

CASE STUDY

Sarah is a newly appointed team manager in a social work team, having been promoted from a social work role in the same team. She has considerable practice experience and skills which identified her as someone who had the potential for a management role. Although she had a good insight into the work of the team manager based on her relationship with her previous line manager, she is surprised at the range and variety of demands she is now having to meet in her first management post. She feels comfortable working with her team colleagues and supporting their practice and maintaining relationships with a range of external organisations that work in partnership with her service. But she also finds she is expected to respond urgently to the demands of senior managers for information, as part of the requirement for the collection of performance indicators, and to participate in strategic planning meetings, as well as manage a range of staff and financial resources within the limits set by her line manager. She now has to balance the demands of supporting and managing practice with those of strategic and resource management.

ACTIVITY 9.1

When you are on placement arrange to talk to the team manager and ask them about the demands that management places on them and the range of tasks they are expected to achieve. Tell them you have been reading about how the management of social care has changed and ask them how these changes have impacted on their work as a manager. This will give you an insight into their work and help you understand the multiple pressures on them and why they have to balance the demands for services with resources available to them.

Comment

I hope that you have now got a better insight into the work of your manager and understood some of the many pressures they experience stemming from the wide-ranging agenda that managers have to respond to. How your line manager is balancing these demands, in responding to the managerialist pressures of the organisation, and at the same time ensuring that they are able to create time and space to work with both individual social workers and the team will in the end be the test of the overall effectiveness of the service.

Part two: managing your relationship with your manager

We suggested that first line managers have a crucial role in supporting you and providing opportunities for you to engage in work-based learning through opportunities to reflect on your practice. If you are to gain from these opportunities it is important that you develop a relationship with your manager that meets both your needs. Your relationship is one where you have the choice to be passive and succumb to being managed, or to develop an active approach to managing your manager. Managers do not just manage other people, they are managed themselves through the actions of their staff. Developing your skills in managing your relationship with your manager can result where both of you can benefit and in turn the service can become more effective.

Relating to your manager's world

Try to understand you manager's role, the demands on them, and how you can help them achieve their aims. Recognise that your manager is dependent on you, just as much as you are dependent on them. Some of the things you can do to increase your understanding of your manager and their role are to:

- be aware of the pressures and demands on your manager;

- understand some of the constraints they are working under that limit their ability to make decisions about resources that meet your recommendations;

- understand why they may not always be available for consultation as a result of the pressures on them to respond to a wide range of agendas;

- focus on possible solutions rather than appearing to challenge their authority, so that there is a win–win outcome with the desired end obtained without you or your manager losing face.

An important part of successfully managing your relationship with your manager is your own confidence in communicating effectively and adopting an assertive approach. If you are able to communicate assertively it is more likely you will meet your own needs, but also gain the respect of your manager. In turn your manager is likely to feel more confident about your practice if they see you as a practitioner who takes your development seriously and strives to develop a relationship which is effective at both managerial and practice levels.

CASE STUDY

Paul has had a good experience of supervision while a student, where his practice assessor challenged him to take increasing responsibility for his own development as he neared the end of his degree. He is meeting with Sarah to establish the arrangements for supervision and the support he wants her to provide for him. He is conscious of the demands on her time, but wants to ensure that he will be able to use the supervision sessions to support his practice, to critically reflect on his interventions with service users, and also

CASE STUDY continued

opportunities to discuss his wider professional development. In preparation for this first meeting he has spent some time identifying his needs and what he would ideally like the supervision sessions to provide. In this way he is adopting a proactive approach to his own development, which will be welcomed by Sarah, who wants her team members to actively manage their own development with her support.

How you manage your relationship with your line manager will be crucial to your future development. If you can establish a relationship where you both adopt an approach that recognises the value of a reflective learning and questions current practice which has become habitual or is claimed to be 'best practice', the more strategies you will develop over time that enable you to respond to the demands made on you and your service.

Actions that are likely to increase your potential for success include:

- being clear about your role and taking responsibility for your own learning;

- developing yourself to meet the demands of your practice;

- identifying your personal strengths and weaknesses and what you need to do to improve your practice;

- being open to changing your behaviour as a result of feedback from your manager and other colleagues;

- recognising when you need help or support and asking for it;

- giving honest and constructive feedback;

- checking when you are not clear about your manager's statements or behaviour;

- stating your own position openly – clearly expressing your thoughts and feelings.

Part three: creating a learning environment to support practice

We have seen that a particular role and function of first line managers is to promote and sustain practice standards through a knowledge of statutory requirements, external standards and organisational procedures, combined with support for individual practitioners and teams through individual and team supervisory activities (Kearney, 2004). The starting point for ensuring that practice standards are achieved is through a manager's knowledge about how practice should be undertaken, how services are best delivered and being able and willing to share this knowledge with staff. Rosen (2000) argues that managers can best achieve this through 'modelling practice', with staff doing what managers do, rather than what they say should be done. One way that this can be achieved is through the first line manager acting as a professional consultant to the team – consulted about what could be done (methods of intervention) or what should be done (meeting statutory or procedural requirements).

In order to create and sustain an atmosphere in which continuous learning and professional development can take place, it is important that the manager promotes their own learning and development of reflective practice and in turn is more receptive to the development of reflection in colleagues (Thompson, 2000). The first line manager is in a key position to influence the development of high standards of practice. To achieve this requirement managers need to understand how practice should be carried out and be up to date with knowledge-based practice developments.

The importance of the workplace as a setting for learning with the demands and challenges of practice – solving problems, improving quality or coping with change, growing out of the interaction with colleagues – is central to the notion of reflective learning, and Eraut (2001) has identified the appointment and the development of first line managers as one the most important mechanisms for promoting learning in an organisation. Just as the appointment of first line managers and their professional behaviour influence how staff practise, so will the standards managers set for themselves. Darvill (1997), writing about the facilitation of work-based learning, sees this as influenced to a great extent by the manager's own style of working and how much they are seen to value this aspect of their role. He sees the first line manager possessing influence in promoting a vision of the team and work setting as a learning culture, adopting a strategic approach to the development of individuals and the team.

Some of the ways managers can encourage continuous learning

Managers have an important role in relation to continuous learning – first they can see themselves as learners. They are the most visible member of the staff team, with the most complex set of roles, and therefore set an important example to staff. Then they can facilitate continuous staff learning through a range of activities:

- a starting point is declaring the importance they place on their own learning;

- actively using team meetings, supervision and case reviews as a way of asking awkward questions of everyone, about the effectiveness of practice, and encouraging receptivity to new ideas;

- striking a balance between encouraging staff to take risks in testing solutions, but remaining accountable for minimising risk to service users;

- encouraging staff to trust the freedom of the learning process in being open about their professional fears, and perhaps where they feel their practice falls below their own professional standards;

- recognising that some learning may reinforce bad habits or questionable practice. Positive learning demands a willingness to question habits, to experiment and use time to reflect and develop new ways of seeing.

(Based on Darvill, 1997)

RESEARCH SUMMARY

The Chartered Institute of Personnel and Development (CIPD) Training and Development Survey (2004) found that the three most important activities in helping employees learn effectively were the building of a culture in the organisation supportive of learning, ensuring managers have the skills and are committed to supporting learning and development, and that employees are given time to participate in learning opportunities in the workplace. The commitment to learning at the most senior levels in organisations was seen as crucial in order to create a learning culture, alongside an environment where individuals felt able to make mistakes and learn from them, and where they were encouraged to question, take risks and try new things. The survey also found that employees believed they learnt most effectively from workplace learning opportunities, with coaching and mentoring also considered highly effective ways of helping individuals to learn. An aspect of this report that resonates with Gould and Baldwin's (2004) work on social work and learning organisations, is the need for employees to be given time to learn at work. Gould and Baldwin describe the difficulties practitioners found in persuading their organisations to grant space for reflective activities, and without these opportunities there was little chance of developing strategies for effective practice (CIPD, 2004).

Opportunities for using reflective practice

First line managers and their staff have a range of opportunities available to them where reflection on practice can take place. The following examples are provided to give you some idea about the possibilities open to you and your manager.

Supervision

Supervision provides a unique opportunity for supporting staff and providing a context for the development of reflective practice. Supervision most usefully needs to address four key functions:

- *responsibility for managing the supervisee's work;*
- *providing emotional and practical support;*
- *helping the supervisee's professional development;*
- *acting as a channel of communication between frontline staff and middle and senior management.*

(Morrison, 1993)

It is through the process of reflection in supervisory sessions that professional learning can take place, both by analysing the explanations and the evidence on which assessments and interventions were based and identifying where there are developmental needs in relation to practice. This requires the supervisor and supervisee to separate out what went well and what hindered practice interventions, so that they can first articulate for themselves and then communicate to service users what has underpinned their assessments and their choice of interventions, and thereby use supervision to provide accountability to people using the service as well as governance of the service (Cunningham, 2004). It is here in the supervisory setting that reflection on action can take place – you have the opportunity to reflect on recent practice following a particular intervention, learning from it by connecting thoughts and actions.

Gould (1996) argues that reflective learning operates through an understanding of professional knowledge developed through practice and systematic analysis of experience. Using this approach, reflective practice involves drawing selectively and appropriately on our professional knowledge base, integrating theory and practice, rather than relying on theory to provide ready-made answers, by being prepared to learn from experience by reflecting on it and being open to new ideas.

Staff in social care agencies benefit from the process knowledge that can be learnt from good supervision. This is where managers focus on the developmental aspects of supervision, although this can often be neglected under the pressures of work, with the time and opportunity to share and reflect on practice – the time for interactive debate and development of critical thinking skills – often neglected by the need to focus on the micro-details of individual casework (Sawdon and Sawdon, 1995). The pressures on first line managers to monitor the performance of staff and focus on the need to meet quantifiable outcomes, with its concern that workers' activities are based on uniform standards, risks undermining staff's ability to adjust, to think and to create.

This approach also risks practitioners developing what Thompson (2000) describes as a routinised approach to practice where they come to rely on routines that are applied in complex and demanding situations, with routine approaches applied inappropriately, that stems from (among other things) the use of untested assumptions, relying on stereotypes and missing opportunities for learning and professional development. It is the line manager's job to ensure that a team or organisational culture does not develop and encourage a routinised approach in spite of organisational pressures towards conformity.

The focus on ensuring that practice meets regulatory requirements has wider risks. The successful organisations seem to operate on the edge of their competence, where workers are continually engaging with the unknown and the unknowable. This view is reinforced by Ixer's (1999) comment that reflective practice recognises the *swampy lowlands of human distress* where professional decision-making is far more complex than the current obsession with occupational standards and competences would suggest.

ACTIVITY 9.2

- *Reflect on your recent experience of supervision. How far did the session address the four main functions of supervision?*

- *If the session did not meet your needs, can you identify what aspect of the session was unsuccessful?*

- *Was it to do with the location?*

- *Was it to do with the structure?*

- *Was it to do with the content?*

ACTIVITY 9.2 *continued*

- *Was it to do with the process?*
- *Was it related to your manager's contribution?*
- *Was it related to your own contribution?*
- *What could your manager do to ensure the next session is more successful?*
- *What could you do to ensure your next session is more successful?*

Comment

This activity should have helped you judge the effectiveness of your supervision sessions and whether they are meeting your needs. If they are not, it could be concerned with a lack of clarity about the expectations that both you and your supervisor have about supervision and its purpose. A contract that sets out the purpose, processes, practical arrangements and expectations of supervision can help create a more effective supervisory relationship in the future.

Consultation

A second area that provides an opportunity for reflective practice is consultation. This is a problem-solving process where you can use your manager as a consultant. The difference between consultation and supervision is that it can be a one-off event and that you (as consultee) set the agenda and that your manager's role (as consultant) is to facilitate your working through a specific issue that concerns you. You need the experience and expertise of another person who can offer the help you need. You can of course use other people in your team, or in the wider service if you feel they have the necessary expertise to assist you.

Using Schein's (1987) approach to consultation, it is a process where your manager, acting in the role of consultant, works collaboratively with you in a manner that enables you to develop your own assessment of the issue and use your skills to act.

The process involves:

- stage one: active listening on the part of the manager as they encourage you to describe the issue that concerns you, and try to understand the issues from your perspective;

- stage two: diagnostic intervention which focuses on helping you to think about what is going on in the situation through reflection on previous actions or interventions;

- stage three: action alternatives is the stage when the focus shifts to what you want to consider in terms of action and that you can begin to describe action that will follow the consultation.

Ideally your manager will ask you questions which provoke you to form your own ideas as to why events have occurred and what might be done. This also takes the pressure off the manager of having to be the expert and provide solutions, and in turn helps you to come to a judgement about the issue and to learn something about the process of problem-solving.

In this way consultation provides a valuable opportunity to reflect on a practice situation and through a problem-solving process build your confidence to act in the future, but also to experience using the expertise of your manager in a non-managerial relationship.

CASE STUDY

Paul has been asked to take responsibility for working with a service user where a succession of workers has tried a range of interventions without success. He is concerned that his intervention will lead to similar frustrations and has asked his team manager Sarah if she will help him work through some of the issues and discuss various approaches to work with the service user. She agrees to meet with him and discuss his concerns. Her approach is not to suggest how he approaches the service user, but to explore the issues, probe and test his assumptions and support him to make his own decisions about the options he could consider when he meets the service user for the first time. In this way she hopes to help him become more confident in his practice, but also to model an approach to problem-solving where her team members do not become dependent on her for answers to problems, but develop confidence in their own problem-solving abilities.

To work effectively in a consultative relationship it is important that you take responsibility for how you want to work with your manager (or another member of staff) in a consultative role, including:

- to openly share your concerns about the issue and why you need help in thinking through your approach;

- accepting constructive feedback from your manager;

- to participate in problem-solving and not to expect just to be told what to do;

- to reflect on the issues and explore the options open to you;

- to take responsibility for implementing the action plan you have decided on.

Reviewing and evaluating interventions

A further opportunity to review practice and in turn reflect on the effectiveness of interventions can be undertaken by evaluating practice. Although supervisory sessions and consultation provide settings for reflection, other contexts are also important opportunities to develop these skills. Review and evaluation are parts of the five stages of systematic practice of assessment: intervention, review, termination and evaluation (Thompson, 2000).

Reviewing practice enables the practitioner and their manager to explore current approaches and whether adjustments need to be made in the plan, or radically different tactics need to be used. A service user's situation can change over time and assessment may need to change too as an initial assessment may have been based on partial information. It is important then that practice is reviewed periodically so that adjustments can be made to the intervention plan. A consequence of not reviewing practice regularly is that time, effort and energy can be wasted because the intervention is misdirected. The review gives you an opportunity to amend or confirm your plan of intervention.

Once an intervention is completed there is the opportunity to learn from the intervention and evaluate what worked and what was less successful, and what can be learned from the process. This process should take you back to the initial assessment and your original objectives, how far you were able to meet these and what was not achieved, given the time, resources and priorities (Thompson, 2000).

Evaluation of interventions is also important, both in terms of the intervention overall and its impact, but also in relation to the increasing pressure on organisations to review the effectiveness of their services as a result of external inspections, for example Best Value reviews and other demands regarding increasing the efficiency of service provision. A key part of evaluation is the need for social workers to understand that it can enhance the effectiveness of practice and build accountability and transparency into practice. From a wider perspective it is increasingly expected by those who fund services and those who use them, so that together evaluating interventions and outcomes enables social workers to become more effective and efficient (Alston and Bowles, 2003). Evaluation is also an important element in social workers developing a research-mindedness approach to their practice, and countering the risks when so much practice inevitably *happens on the hoof, without the opportunity for critical evaluation* (Gould and Bradshaw, 2004, p46). It is therefore important that you value and appreciate the contribution that research can make to developing more effective forms of intervention, which can include researching your own practice to improve it and ensure it is at the forefront of best practice.

At an organisational level first line managers are required to provide numerical data for senior managers, who in turn have to respond to government demands for statistical information on how a service is meeting national targets. Although the introduction of regulations and standard setting can provide an important stimulus to address neglected service issues, it also means that managers and practitioners focus on a narrow range of targeted activities with the risks of a routinised approach to practice to the detriment of service users, practitioners and their organisations (Statham, 2004). We can see that review and evaluation play an important part in the development of practice and provide an opportunity for social work to demonstrate its effectiveness and respond to the attacks that undermine the confidence and morale of staff, stemming from a managerially-driven agenda.

RESEARCH SUMMARY

The Management of Practice Expertise Project undertaken by the National Institute for Social Work had as one of its aims to identify what kind of approaches to management enabled staff to develop and sustain their practice expertise. This was conducted through a survey of supervision arrangements and policies in social services departments, a study of a group of practice sites and conferences and workshops that brought together managers and practitioners to explore the relationship between management, supervision and practice development. In a discussion paper published as part of the research, it found that first line managers were vital to the practice and service delivery of an organisation and that they were the keystones between senior management and frontline staff, their team and other teams and between the agency and other services and individuals. The key role of the first line manager was concerned with holding together the different

(continued)

RESEARCH SUMMARY *continued*

worlds and avoiding the damaging fragmentation if these different worlds did not maintain relationships with each other. Other important roles were the deployment of resources and ensuring that standards in practice were set and maintained, that staff were supported when engaging in complex and demanding practice, and that they were continually developed in knowledge-based practice. This is particularly achieved where the managers model practice and their work is visible, for example in residential settings, and where they act as consultants to team members, playing the role of crucial opinion leaders (Rosen, 2000).

Conclusion

Developing an effective working relationship with your manager is a crucial part of your development as a professional social worker. How you use this relationship will be important in defining how far you move beyond comfortable openness that is bounded by shared mental models to a position where you surface more of your biases and interpretations about practice that can challenge you and lead to real change (Senge, 2006).

Of course much of the success of this relationship will also depend on your manager and how far they have developed their own skills in reflecting on practice and are able to move beyond defensive routines that have become such a powerful part of the managerialist ethos in many services. Ideally you and your manager need to be ready to discuss practice that acknowledges different interpretations and builds capacity both at practitioner and organisational level to deal with the complexities of social work practice.

C H A P T E R   S U M M A R Y

- The role of first line managers has changed significantly from the traditional focus on supporting practice to one that more closely resembles the general manager, with responsibilities for the efficient management of resources, the effective performance of staff and the achievement of the strategic goals of the organisation.

- First line managers are increasingly having to balance the demands of the organisation with the need to ensure the maintenance and support of practice as a result of the managerialist ethos in social care organisations.

- You can significantly influence your relationship with your line manager through the adoption of a proactive and positive approach to managing this important relationship.

- Working with your manager to develop a mutually satisfactory working relationship can benefit you both, and in turn service users and the wider organisation, as your practice improves and develops.

- First line managers have a wide range of methods available to them to support your development, through supervision, consultation and evaluation of your practice. Each has the potential to use reflection as a means of widening your understanding of practice.

- Knowing how to take advantage of the different techniques available can help you decide how your manager can best support you.

- Working with your manager to explore the complexities of practice means a degree of openness and willingness to challenge assumptions that can be uncomfortable and threatening, and open your mental models to deeper examination.

FURTHER READING

Gould, N and Baldwin, M (2004) *Social work, critical reflection and the learning organization.* Aldershot: Ashgate.
This book provides a detailed exploration, with case examples, of the concept of a learning organisation and how social care services need to be structured and managed if they are to provide the context for continuous development and organisational learning.

Statham, D (ed) (2004) *Managing front line practice in social care.* London: Jessica Kingsley Publishers.
This book provides a valuable insight into how managers can support practice, emphasising knowledge-based practice and professional development.

Chapter 10

Reflective practice for collaborative working

Janet McCray

ACHIEVING A SOCIAL WORK DEGREE

This chapter will enable you to become familiar with the following National Occupational Standards.
Key Role 2: Plan, carry out, review and evaluate social work practice, with individuals, families, carers, groups communities and other professionals
- Interact to achieve change and development and to improve life opportunities
Key Role 5: Manage and be accountable, with supervision and support, for your own social work practice within your organisation
- Work within multi-disciplinary and multi-organisational teams, networks and systems
- Contribute to evaluating the effectiveness of the team, network or system
- Deal constructively with disagreements and conflict within relationships
Key Role 6: Demonstrate professional competence in social work practice
- Work within agreed standards of social work practice and ensure own professional development
- Manage complex ethical issues, dilemmas and conflicts
- Contribute to the promotion of best social work practice
It will also introduce you to the following standards as set out in the social work subject benchmarking statement.
3.1.1 Social work services and service users
- The relationship between agency policies, legal requirements and professional boundaries in shaping the nature of services provided in inter-disciplinary contexts and the issues associated with working across professional boundaries and within interdisciplinary groups
3.1.2 The service delivery context
- The contribution of different approaches to management, leaderership and quality in public and independent public services
3.1.3 Values and ethics
- Conceptual links between codes of ethics, regulation of professional conduct and management of potential conflicts generated by codes of different professionals
3.1.5 The nature of social work practice
- The factors and processes that facilitate effective inter-disciplinary, inter-professional and inter-agency collaboration and partnership
- The processes of reflection and evaluation including familiarity with the range of approaches for evaluating welfare outcomes, and their significance for the development of practice and the practitioner
3.1.6 Skills in working with others
- Act co-operatively with others
- Liaising and negotiating across differences such as organisational and professional boundaries

Introduction

Collaborative working with a range of partners is part of daily professional practice. Recent policy changes, for example within *Putting People First* (DoH, 2007) and *High Quality Care for All* (DoH, 2008), have increased the scope, type and range of partnerships. For social workers much of this collaborative practice has taken place within an interprofessional context; however, the range of professional networks and the nature of partnerships for collaboration are shifting, and require new ways of working. At the same time, constant challenges presented by agency boundaries and limited resources remain and the pace of change is unprecedented. Emerging and new partnerships place further demands on the professional leadership role necessary to offer good models of service delivery. One consequence is an increased emphasis on the leadership and managerial skills of social care practice. For social workers and other professionals the result may be a need to re-evaluate their leadership strategies and managerial strengths in order to work more effectively. This chapter explores the use of reflection as an integral part of this process to assist in effective leadership supported through the application of a practice learning tool.

Overview

Throughout this book you will have been reading about and exploring the concept of reflective practice. By now you should have a good understanding of its meaning and application and usefulness as a means to enhance your social work practice. For this chapter based on leadership for collaborative working, planning prior to action and 'reflection on action' (Schön, 1983) with emphasis on evaluation following an event or intervention, are likely to be the most significant form of reflection used. Collaborative working can be a complex process and leading collaboration even more so. In this chapter the aim is to demonstrate how reflection can be of real value in developing practice and assisting thinking about the collaborative working arena. Bulman and Schutz (2004) observe that *By engaging in reflection people are usually engaging in a period of thinking in order to examine often complex experiences or situations. This period of thinking allows the individual to make sense of an experience, liken the experience to other similar experiences and to place it in context.* A range of activities is offered here to explore reflection in collaborative practice with the hope that when you are faced with the challenge of leading collaborative practice you will be able to *Separate out the various influencing factors and come to a reasoned decision or course of action* (Bulman and Schutz, 2004).

ACTIVITY 10.1

Questions to ask yourself at the beginning of this chapter

- *What do I know about collaborative working and leadership roles?*

- *How successful has the collaborative leadership role been for me?*

- *Can reflective practice help me be more effective?*

What is collaborative working?

Collaborative working is used in a range of sectors in the community from business to social and health care. A number of terms are used in the literature to define collaborative working and many are used interchangeably to describe it. Quinney (2006, p11) offers a lexicon of terms used in social work practice and for further reading, her book *Collaborative practice in social work* (2006) in the Learning Matters series explores the subject in depth.

A simple definition of collaborative working is *A respect for other professionals and service users and their skills and from this starting point, an agreed sharing of authority, responsibility and resources aimed at specific outcomes or actions, and gained through cooperation and consensus.*

Loxley (1997, cited in McCray, 2006) describes collaboration as *work across boundaries, work with difference*. For many professionals this means working in different ways with different team members, usually to create change. For example, the implementation of *Every Child Matters* (2004) has increased and made more formal the links between social work and education agencies. The need to take on different and more holistic responsibilities for the care of children created by legislation has meant professionals may be working to new and unforeseen objectives set by government and requiring implementation by professional organisations or agencies. It is unlikely that any one professional group or agency could achieve these responsibilities alone. Hence throughout all practice intervention, collaboration is vital to ensure all professionals are working with each other and with children and families to meet these needs. To be effective, collaboration must involve the pooling of knowledge, skills and resources to achieve the same shared vision.

Here are some other definitions of collaboration:

> *A process that enables independent individuals and organisations to combine their human and material resources so they can accomplish objectives they are unable to bring about alone.*
>
> (Kanter, 1994, p96)

Gray writes:

> *A process through which parties who see different aspects of a problem can explore constructively their differences and search for solutions that go beyond their differences and search for solutions that go beyond their own limited vision of what is possible.*
>
> (Gray, 1989, p5)

More recently, Ansari and Phillips (2001, p19) describe collaboration as: *An advanced shared vision.* From a social and health care perspective, Percy Smith observes: *Agencies working together in a wide variety of different ways to pursue a common goal whilst also pursuing organisational goals* (Percy Smith, 2005, p 24).

Taylor, et al. (2006, p215), in their research review of partnership working, note that *there are a plethora of terms to be grappled with, including participation and partnership, involvement and collaboration as well as interprofessional, interdisciplinary, multiprofessional shared or joint practice to name but a few.* They continue to note that only a minority of writers in the social work field explicitly define partnership working, nor do the potential tensions it creates receive much coverage in the social work literature (Taylor et al., 2006).

Often collaborative working forms an element of multiprofessional and multi-agency teamwork, (Taylor et al., 2006). The term 'multi-agency' is used to describe the involvement of a range of services and professionals in the delivery of health and social care to an individual (McCray, 2006). Multiprofessional practice has been defined by Pollard, Sellman and Senior (2005) *as practice between different professional groups but not necessarily including collaboration.* For example, social workers and nurses agreeing on support with a family but then working separately with the family to provide it. Inter-professional practice is described by Biggs (1997) as that between different professional groups or within teams that have different disciplines within them. This may involve collaboration (Pollard, et al., 2005).

Collaboration, as Biggs (1999) notes, *refers to relations between different agencies and organisations* and with professionals representing a range of care sectors and groups. Key themes include (Biggs, 1999, p18):

- a holistic approach to care;

- focused use of resources to meet goals and outcomes;

- the minimising of the number of professional interventions for service users and their families;

- better and more effective communication.

To achieve good collaboration a number of challenges must be faced and overcome.

ACTIVITY 10.2

What does collaborative working involve and what barriers might prevent effective collaborative working?

Spend a few minutes thinking about the core elements involved and then list the knowledge and skills required together with barriers that could prevent effective collaboration.

Comment

You may have included the following in response to the question 'what does collaborative working involve?':

- Making time to get to know other professionals and their roles and how they may be evolving in new contexts.

- Thinking about language and terms used and their relevance and meaning to other professionals or workers.

- Exploring your own prejudices about other professional groups and their models of practice.

- Reflecting on values and not making assumptions about shared beliefs of views.

- Being clear about resources and their impact on collaboration.

- Being confident about your professional practice and ability in the collaborative working role.

- Being credible – delivering as promised to action plans and keeping others involved of progress.

- Gaining consensus on leadership and accountability in a specific practice situation.

When thinking about barriers to effective collaboaration, you may have included:

- unclear leadership and accountability for the case;

- resource issues around funding or costs;

- conflict between professionals;

- power differences between those involved;

- lack of knowledge of organisations or their boundaries.

Leadership in collaborative working

As you may have found through reading and reflecting on the chapter so far, collaborative working, whilst of great value, can also be a complex process, whilst leading collaborative working may be even more so. What sort of leadership style is appropriate? To consider this in more detail we need to think about leadership in a broader sense.

Designing, developing and evaluating leadership styles, types and models have been a major task of researchers and practitioners in all sectors of service delivery. As the literature demonstrates, the popularity of leadership styles or types tends to reflect a particular political or socioeconomic view. Jasper (2005, p3), in her introduction to leadership in the twenty-first century, cites Avery (2004, p7) who observes that the challenge for leadership is to *operate under rapidly mutating circumstances, which require a rethink of paradigms of leadership both in theory and practice.*

Traditional transactional leadership, that is, leadership by goals and reward and underpinned by social exchange theory, has been the most frequently applied leadership style in public-sector management. Social exchange theory can be described as a negotiated relationship between two parties at work, resulting in the payment or reward for completion of a particular task, project or intervention. In the transactional leadership model leaders and managers set goals and objectives whilst workers are rewarded or penalised based on their progress towards achieving them. Usually these are individually identified and achieved. However, new models of service delivery with an emphasis on team or group collaboration may result in the need for a broader range of relationships and partnerships, as group or team goals and accountabilities make a reliance solely on the transactional leadership model less feasible and ineffective. Hence the current popularity of the transformational leader (Burns, 1978). Bate (1994) describes one of the responsibilities of a leader as being that of *creating the conditions to release potential energy*, thus describing this facilitation role which is a key characteristic of transformational leadership. In this model leaders share goals with workers and explore together in groups or teams methods and strategies for achieving them. Thus all work together to gain rewards. Odegard and Strype (2009, p286) emphasise that effective collaboration requires active leadership of groups with organisations. A further critical element of transformational leadership is responsiveness to change whilst constantly developing new networks and practising effectively (Hackett and Spurgeon, 1998). When times are uncertain there can be increased stress for workers. Gouva, et al's (2009, p1441) study of nurses showed that leaders could support the well-being of their teams through enabling greater collaboration between education and practice with reflection being an important tool. The use of emotional intelligence is important. Anderson and West (1998, p235) offer a taxonomy of transforming practices which include communication, counselling and consultation underpinned by the development of self-awareness and self-management. A key value of the transformational leader is that of ensuring and enabling the personal and professional growth in expertise and skill of the team and its members.

Leadership in practice

As a social work student you may be at the start of your leadership or managerial career, or you could have had previous experience of managing others in an earlier job or work role. Think about your own role in practice. Whilst on placement, what models or styles of leadership have you used in a formal or informal way? Did any particular style feel most comfortable or create more tension? Some people are drawn to facilitative leadership styles based on good social skills and the positivity of engaging others in the change process. Has this been your experience? Alternatively in some situations a more transactional or direct style may be most valid and comfortable. As part of your practice supervision, have you had assessor or peer feedback on your effectiveness? In your student life have you been a group or course representative? Have these experiences offered skills and strategies that may be effective for leading collaborative working? You may have found you enjoy a combination of styles, or a preference for one approach that felt most effective, just as you may feel the need to build up more experience before stating a preference.

ACTIVITY 10.3

Good leadership observed

In your social work training you may have come across people you consider to have good leadership skills. For example, your practice assessor could have offered valuable skills and intervention in managing you and your university link. Alternatively you may have observed a team manager supporting a team to work to a new set of performance indicators or targets, over a period of time. Whatever the setting, how were these demonstrated?

Comment

You may have included:

- sensitive communication skills;
- vision and focus shared with others;

- ability to inspire and motivate others;
- honesty and trust in relationships;
- provider of clear frameworks for practice and feedback.

Examples of leadership in practice

A range of leadership strategies are available to managers in the practice setting. Earlier these were defined as that of the traditional individual goal-focused approach of transactional leadership through to the currently popular transformational style useful in team work settings. You may have used or been exposed to either or both of these models. In the next part of the chapter examples of each style and their use are presented.

Transactional leadership

The problem In team A, all professionals manage their own caseloads and ensure these are up to date. Currently team A is adequately resourced and there have been no members on long-term sickness leave nor are there frozen posts, which might have put pressure on other team A members. On reviewing a number of individual service user profiles held as a caseload by a staff member, you note several who have not had assessments or visits for some time.

The response You are not aware of a strong reason for this from the workers' or team A's perspective. You as the manager first check this is the case and then decide on a date for rectifying this, and inform the staff member of your decision.

Transformational leadership

The problem At a team meeting, a team member notes that changes to the configuration of the local primary care trust mean that some nursing professionals will be moving base and taking on new roles. As a leader you think this may be significant for future working and alliances particularly around supporting children with disability.

The response You ask the group what the issues might be and what new strategies might be required to ensure continued collaboration. Following discussion a plan is drawn up by the team to explore the issues and a leader (not yourself) is identified and agreed by the team to take this forward.

Collaborative working

Both models may be effective in collaboration, especially when results or outputs are viewed by other professionals or workers as evidence of commitment and credibility. For example, a professional who does not regularly review her caseload will not be viewed positively by others; hence it may be appropriate to use a hierarchical or transactional leadership model here. Equally when new situations happen and changes in working patterns occur, a different approach and response to problem-solving with shared leadership based on a transformational style may be more effective.

Using reflection to assist in the effective leadership of collaborative working

Up to this point, brief explorations of collaborative working and leadership have been presented and you have had the opportunity to reflect on your current collaborative leadership role and style. It's time to think more about enhancing collaboration through reflection.

The following framework has been developed to act as a guide, model or toolkit for practice (McCray, 2003a and b). At its simplest it acts as an express checklist to focus thinking or action before, during or after a collaborative working intervention. However, it may also be used as a tool for deeper reflection on practice, helping to support exploration of a number of components of collaborative working from a specific starting point. (See Figure 10.1.)

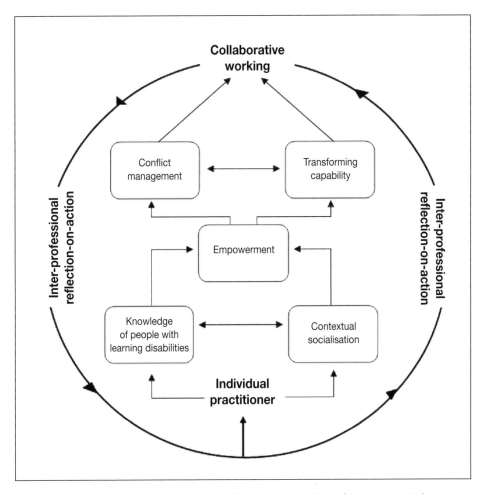

Figure 10.1 A conceptual framework for collaborative working (McCray, 2003a)

About the framework

The components in the framework were originally developed through research with nurses and social workers in the field of learning disability (McCray, 2003b). Through exploring practice activity around multiprofessional working key concepts or components of good practice were developed. These components were placed in order, drawing on practitioners' experience and the research evidence available. For example, the practitioners in the original study had suggested that it was no use working to empower service users without knowledge of the person themselves and the context in which the empowerment was needed. If we looked at the literature on collaboration and inter-agency working, a key factor in leading teams is credibility (Hudson, 1999). If time is not taken to gain knowledge and understanding of a situation, then when asked to support or intervene the contribution may not be credible. Thus a leader would not gain support to consider changing responses or in the facilitation of the service user's actions to make change for themself.

Only though attention to the person (Knowledge of the person Component 1) and the context (Contextual socialisation Component 2) is empowerment (the third component of the framework) of the practitioner or service users and carers or other staff likely. The key to this attention is reflection on action (Component 6 Inter-professional reflection-on-action), which Mantell (2007) in Chapter 5 of this book describes as an outcome-driven activity or review. In this model this process is undertaken at each stage of the collaborative working action with a focus on what the individual may have done differently (if anything) at each point through to what the individual might need to change for future intervention, or strategies.

Participants in the original study questioned the use of power in inter-professional collaboration. They observed that without being and feeling empowered themselves, they were unable to empower others or feel comfortable sharing power with service users and carers. They suggested that transforming leaders work towards a basis for practice underpinned by mutual, value-focused agreement in order to create positive social change. Only though addressing and recognising power issues (Component 3 Empowerment component), can the practitioner begin to create and plan for real change (Component 4 Transforming capability) and design and apply new methods for recognising and responding to any conflict created (Component 5 Conflict management). Once again attention is paid to the effectiveness of these strategies using reflection-on-action.

Using the framework

CASE STUDY

You are the lead social worker supporting Sophia, aged 15, and her family. Sophia has physical and learning disabilities and lives at home in a supportive and close-knit family.

Sophia has had good educational and children's service health care support through her life, but as she draws near to school-leaving age and moves towards adult services, she and her family have been expressing concerns about the future, and the opportunities for continued health care support and potential employment opportunities. At a recent review

---

CASE STUDY *continued*

meeting Sophia and her family voiced these concerns and the lack of future plans in place for her transition to more adult-focused services. Major worries were gaps in terms of links with adult health services for monitoring and treatment of her physical disability, and access to learning-disability agencies' support.

Following this meeting you contacted your professional colleagues in health about Sophia's future needs and provision before a further meeting with Sophia and her family.

ACTIVITY *10.4*

Preparation for collaboration

As you prepare for the meeting with health colleagues, you use the reflective framework to help you.

Your starting point is your current knowledge of Sophia and her family (Component 1). You ask yourself a number of questions related to them:

Have you adequate knowledge about their views on needs for the future?

Is this knowledge recent or does it require reviewing? Are Sophia and her family happy for you to act on their behalf?

Have you enough knowledge to act with credibility?

Given exploration of the knowledge element, you reflect on the context (Component 2) in which multiprofessional collaboration is taking place. You ask yourself a number of questions. These might include:

What is the impact of Sophia's transition into adult services on the family?

Are there any social or economic factors involved?

Will more or a different form of support be required if Sophia leaves full-time education?

Am I familiar with acute health care service processes or do I have appropriate multiprofessional links to facilitate?

Would there be new resource issues to work through, as Sophia has a number of health care needs?

What is the current situation like for others in transition using these local health care services?

In exploring these questions you might reflect also on your preparation for leadership in this context. What sorts of links do you have with other professionals in adult services in health care and have they been effective? What factors have influenced their effectiveness? For example, have you worked together before with success and thus respect the professional knowledge and skill of the other professional, or has there been conflict created by a pressure on resources? You may have worked together on a project group with other health care professionals which has given you a mutual interest and previous team-work experience. You may reflect on the impact of these experiences on planning your leadership strategy for this current multiprofessional collaboration.

ACTIVITY **10.5**

Think about your responses to the critical reflection commentary so far. What sorts of questions might you explore in relation to the empowerment component?

Comment

You may have included:

How much involvement has Sophia had in planning her transition to adult services so far?

What role have her family played?

What other professionals are involved in the transition process and what roles do they play?

To what extent are resources an issue in relation to empowerment and choice?

What is my role and where can my power be used most effectively?

As you progress through the model you should be building a picture of your role and leadership strengths and needs in this situation. It may be that this is all very positive and you are affirming your multiprofessional leadership skills and knowledge. Alternatively, there may be areas of development required that the reflective activity is highlighting. For example, your reflection might also be bringing out the conflict that could be present as debates with other professionals get under way. You may need to ask yourself a number of questions about conflict management. These could include the level of safety you feel in a conflict-management situation. This could be dependent on the nature of the conflict being presented. Is it based on resources and who will provide them, or the absence of a viable and appropriate transitional service, creating numerous obstacles to good provision for Sophia? Sometimes interpersonal issues can get in the way of positive thinking and planning. Your decisions around the nature of the conflict should guide you in considering where the conflict should be addressed. It may not be of value for it to take place in the team setting, but in some other arena. On some occasions conflict may be better ignored, but in taking this route a clear and honest exploration of conflict-management models should have taken place, as well as seeking feedback during supervision. Your reflections might include an exploration of the consequences of ignoring the source of conflict, and considering whether you are the most appropriate person to deal with the conflict. In the longer term you may be concerned with the impact of conflict on collaborative working relationships.

Having worked though potential responses to any conflict and its management and decided on a solution, only then are you in a position to create change.

ACTIVITY *10.6*

At this point an action plan can be made and you might reflect on:

How supportive will the team be of your approach and outline plan for Sophia?

What information around resources needs to be highlighted?

What other new skills, networks and/or information do I need?

Can a time frame be put in place?

Are there any team members who may chose not to collaborate?

How close is the likely outcome of the collaborative process to Sophia's family's wishes?

What form of leadership is likely to work to manage the change process?

Finally having worked though all the components of the framework you can return to its starting point and reflect on the effectiveness of your collaborative working leadership and what you have learned.

Using the framework for your practice

ACTIVITY *10.7*

Having seen an example of the framework's use with the case study above, you should now try it out using an example from your own collaborative working caseload. Before you begin this, remind yourself of your responses to the initial questions about your collaborative working leadership style at the beginning of the chapter:

- *What methods do I use currently to reflect on my collaborative working leadership role?*

- *Are they useful in evaluating my practice?*

- *Do I share them openly with others in a formal or informal setting?*

- *How successful are they for me?*

After you have worked through your own case, you might also wish to reflect on your initial responses to the questions about your leadership style in Activity 10.1. Do you think your current methods are effective and successful, or do you need to develop new approaches or tools to support your practice? What did you gain from using the reflective framework and can the framework add to your current methods of reflection and evaluation? Some individuals might not have found the framework useful. If this is the case for you, what other form of tool or resources might help? As we arrive at the final part of this chapter, it is timely to ask yourself what further action you need to take following completion of the activities within it. You might want to undertake further reading around the topics introduced in the chapter or benefit from discussion with your practice assessor or mentor about further development of skills for practice. It may be of interest to search for other tools or strategies to support reflective practice for collaborative activity or reading more about the framework used here. Finally, have you identified areas requiring additional professional development and do you know where to seek it?

CHAPTER SUMMARY

This chapter has introduced collaborative working leadership. It has presented a practical tool to aid reflection on collaborative working leadership using a series of exercises and a case study. Throughout, a number of activities and reflective cues have placed emphasis on your own practice and thinking as a social work practitioner. By reading the chapter you may have gained new insights into your collaborative working role and leadership style and highlighted areas for continuing personal development. Alternatively you may have affirmed your current collaborative working style and reflective activity.

Whichever is the case, what remains certain is that there will be an increasing need for social workers to be equipped with collaborative working leadership skills. Further reflection on the attributes required and your individual readiness for the role will both support and enhance your future professional development.

FURTHER READING

Barett, GS, Ellman, D and Thomas, J (2005) *Interprofessional working for health and social care.* Basingstoke : Palgrave.
This book provides the case for inter-professional working and looks at the impact on a range of professional groups and their practice.

Mullins, L J (2009) *Essentials of management and organisational behaviour.* London: Prentice Hall.
A useful management textbook with examples from health and social care looking at management and leadership in organisations and teams.

Quinney, A (2006) *Collaborative social work practice.* Learning Matters: Exeter.
This book will offer you more detailed information about collaboration in social work practice.

Conclusion

This book has covered a range of topics from the perspective of reflective practice. It has introduced you to the concepts that have informed our understanding of reflective practice and the way knowledge is potentially used by professionals and what you need to consider if you are to become an effective practitioner. By understanding how you can become a more skilled reflective practitioner we hope it will help you narrow the gap between the theory and practice of social work and generate practice-based knowledge that can guide your actions.

Social work deals with people who need practitioners to be responsive and reflective instead of simply carrying out everyday practice in a routine or ritualistic manner. Reflection on practice can help you guard against the risks of 'working on autopilot' in which you follow the same pattern of practice that governs and directs your action. It provides the opportunity to focus on your practice and confront, understand and work towards resolving the contradictions that are inherent in much social work practice.

In the first part of this book (Chapters 1and 2) we have provided you with some of the key concepts that have informed the development of reflective practice, and a range of processes that you can adopt to develop your own skills in reflection on and about your practice, with examples of some of the methods that can be used when you first engage in reflection on your practice, and which you can return to throughout your social work career. In these chapters we have cautioned you about the risks associated with technical and rational assumptions about practice, in situations which are often messy and uncertain, where the value of reflection on and about your practice can help you understand, learn and discover new approaches that reconcile some of the contradictions within social work practice.

The second part has focused on a range of techniques and issues that can be illuminated and enhanced by using techniques of reflection. First, understanding the role of your emotions (Chapter 3) and how emotional intelligence can help you explore more fully your responses to practice issues. This is followed (Chapter 4) by an example of how you can use techniques adapted from cognitive behaviour therapy to examine your own thought patterns and develop more confidence at a personal and practice level. Drawing on recent research (Chapter 5) we examine work with carers that poses important questions about the role of service users and carers in the social work relationship, and alerts you to some of the complex issues involved when you are working in these situations. We then consider (Chapter 6) an area that is important to all social workers, that of working with service users who are hostile and aggressive. Our intention is to demonstrate how you can use reflection to more fully understand risk and minimise professional dangerousness in your practice. We then examined the role of gender in social work (Chapter 7) and some of the key issues that are important to understand as you explore gender both in the student setting and in practice situations. The influence of gender, both in terms of personal identity and the expectations of others were discussed, and their importance in helping you to understand how they may impact on you in practice situations. Finally in this section (Chapter 8), we examine reflective practice from the standpoint of practice placements. This chapter is intended to help you understand how practice assessors approach their task and how you can more fully prepare for your placement through the process of reflection about your practice in partnership with your practice assessor.

The third and final part focuses on management and how reflective practice can be promoted and maintained through a range of management and organisational processes. We first explore the world of the first line manager (Chapter 9) and their crucial role in ensuring that they balance the demands of practice with the demands of the wider organisation, with suggestions of ways you can manage your relationship with your manager, and some of the techniques that you can use to reflect on and about, practice with your manager. Finally we acknowledge (Chapter 10) that social work increasingly takes place in an inter-professional context, and how leadership, at all levels, is essential to effective social work and service delivery. We hope that these two chapters will provide you with a deeper understanding of the world of management and the inter-professional context which you will begin to experience as a student on placement and more fully engage with as your career develops.

We hope you have found this book helpful in providing an insight into how you can develop your practice using concepts and techniques of reflection, and stimulated you to test out approaches to reflection that provide an opportunity to explore your practice with your practice learning assessor. We also hope that once your are qualified you will retain a commitment to reflective practice as part of your continuing professional development, making time to engage in reflection and be willing to challenge current practice where it fails to provide satisfactory answers, recognising that there is no end point to learning for the effective social work practitioner.

References

Chapter 1

Ashford, D, Blake, D and Knott, C (1998) Changing conceptions of reflective practice. *Journal of Interprofessional Care* 12, (1).

Belenky, M, Clinchy, BM, Goldberger, N and Tartule J. (1987) *Women's ways of knowing: The development of self, voice and mind*. New York: Basic Books.

Brookfield, S (1987) *Developing critical thinkers*. Buckingham: Open University Press.

Brown, K and Rutter, L (2006) *Critical thinking for social work*. Exeter: Learning Matters.

Dewey, J (1933) *How we think*. Boston, MA: D. C. Heath.

Dewey, J (1938) *Logic: The theory of inquiry*. Troy, MN: Reinhart and Winston.

Eraut, M (1994) *Developing professional knowledge and competence*. Lewes: Falmer Press.

General Social Care Council (2002) *Code of practice for social care workers and Code of practice for employers of social care workers*. London: GSCC.

Healy, K (2005) *Social work theories in context: Creating frameworks for practice*. Basingstoke: Palgrave Macmillan.

Horner, N (2004) *What is social work? Context and perspectives*. Exeter: Learning Matters.

Ixer, G (1999) There's no such thing as reflection. *British Journal of Social Work*, 29 (6), 13–27.

Jennings, C and Kennedy, E (1996) *The reflective professional in education*. London: Jessica Kingsley Publishers.

Mezirow, J and Karlovic, LN (1992) Fostering critical reflection in adulthood: A guide to transformative and emancipatory learning. *Canadian Journal for the Study of Adult Education*, 6 (1), 86–9.

Moon, J (1999) *Reflection in learning and professional development: Theory and practice*. London: Kogan Page.

Moon, J (2004) *A handbook of reflective and experiential learning: Theory and practice*. London: RoutledgeFalmer.

Nathan, J (2002) The advanced practitioner: Beyond reflective practice. *Journal of Practice Teaching*, 4 (2), 59–84.

Parker, J and Bradley, G (2010) *Social work practice: Assessment, planning, intervention and review*. 3rd edition. Exeter: Learning Matters.

Parton, N (2001) The current state of social work in UK universities: Some personal reflections. *Social Work Education*, 20, 167–74.

Paul, R and Elder, L (2005) *A miniature guide to critical thinking: Concepts and tools.* The Foundation for Critical Thinking, **www.criticalthinking.org**

Reid, W (1994) The empirical practice movement. *Social Service Review*, 69, 165–84.

Rolfe, G, Freshwater, D and Jasper, M (2001) *Critical reflection for nursing and the helping professions*. Basingstoke: Palgrave Macmillan.

Smith, F (1992) *To think in language, learning and education*. London: Routledge.

Tate, S and Sills, M (eds) (2004) *The development of critical reflection in the health professions*. London: Higher Education Academy.

Taylor, C and White, S (2000) *Practising reflexivity in health and welfare: Making knowledge*. Buckingham: Open University Press.

Chapter 2

Boud, D, Hough, R and Walker, D (eds) (1985) *Reflection: Turning experience into learning*. London: Kogan Page.

Boyd, E and Fales, A (1983) Reflective learning: Key to learning from experience. *Journal of Human Psychology*, 23 (2), 94–117.

Cottrell, S (2003) *Skills for success: The personal development planning guide*. Basingstoke: Palgrave Macmillan.

Crisp, BR, Green Lister, P and Dutton, K (2004) *Integrated assessment*. Dundee: Scottish Institute for Excellence in Social Work Education.

Fawcett, M (2005) *Learning through observation*. London: Jessica Kingsley Publishers.

Freud, S (1988) *My three mothers and other passions*. New York: New York University Press.

Honey, P and Mumford, A (1982 and 1992) *The manual of learning styles questionnaire*. Maidenhead: Peter Honey Publications.

Kolb, DA and Fry, R (1975) Towards an applied theory of experiential learning. In Cooper, CL (ed) *Towards and applied theory of group processes*. London: John Wiley.

McConnell, D (2006) *E-learning groups and commmunities*. Maidenhead: McGraw-Hill.

Moon, JA (1999) *Reflection in learning and professional development: Theory and practice*. London: Kogan Page.

Moon, J (2004) *A handbook of reflective and experiential learning: Theory and practice*. London: RoutledgeFalmer.

Progoff, I (1975) *At a journal workshop*. New York: Dialogue House Library.

Rai, L (2006) Owning (up to) reflective writing in social work education. *Social Work Education* 25 (8), 785–97.

Taylor, C (2006) Narrating significant experience: reflective accounts and the production of (self) knowledge. *British Journal of Social Work*, 38, 189–206.

Thompson, N (2002) *Understanding social work: Preparing for practice*. 2nd edition. Basingstoke: Palgrave Macmillan.

Chapter 3

Bailey, R and Brake, M (eds) (1975) *Radical social work*. London: Arnold.

Biestek, F (1961) *The casework relationship*. London: Allen & Unwin.

Bock, G and James, S (1992) *Beyond equality and difference*. London: Palgrave.

Cherniss, C and Goleman, D (2001) *The emotionally intelligent workplace*. San Francisco, CA: Jossey-Bass **www.eiconsortium.org**

Conner, MG (2001) Transference: Are you a biological time machine? *The Source*. Accessed 11.2.07 **www.crisiscounselling.com**

Cooper, A and Lousada, J (2005) *Borderline welfare: Feeling and fear of feeling in modern welfare*. London: Karnac.

Ferguson, H (2005) Working with violence, the emotions and the psycho-social dynamics of child protection: Reflections on the Victoria Climbié case. *Social Work Education*, 24 (7), 781–95.

Gregory, M and Holloway, M (2005) Language and the shaping of social work. *British Journal of Social Work*, 35 (1) 37–53.

Hugman, R (2005) *New approaches to ethics in the caring professions*. Basingstoke: Palgrave.

Laming, H (2003) *The Victoria Climbié inquiry report. Cm5730*. London: The Stationery Office. Crown copyright. **www.victoria-climbié-inquiry.org.uk/fine/report.pdf**

McLannahan, H (2004) *Emotions and mind 6*. Buckingham: Open University Press.

Moon, J (2005) *Critical thinking*. Bristol: Escalate.

Morrow Lindbergh, A (2002) *Gift from the sea*. London: Chatto & Windus.

Pennebaker, J (1997) *Opening up: The healing power of expressing emotions*. New York: Guilford Press.

Pennebaker, J (2007) Writing to heal: A guided journal for recovering from trauma and upheaval. Oakland, CA: New Harbinger Publications.

Ruch, G (2005) Relationship-based practice and reflective practice: holistic approaches to contemporary child care social work. *Child and Family Social Work*, 10, 111–23.

Rustin, M (2005) Conceptual analysis of critical moments in Victoria Climbié's life. *Child and Family Social Work*, 10, 11–19.

Trowell, J and Miles, G (1996) The contribution of observation training to professional development in social work. In G Bridge and G Miles (eds) *On the outside looking in*. London: Central Council for Education and Training in Social Work.

Chapter 4

Beck, J (1995) *Cognitive therapy basics and beyond*. New York: Guilford Press.

Bolton, G (2001) *Reflective practice, writing and professional development*. London: Sage.

Butler, G and Hope, T (2007) *Manage your mind*. 2nd edition. Oxford: Oxford University Press.

Cottrell, S (2005) *Critical thinking skills*. Basingstoke: Palgrave.

Duncan, E and Sheffield, D (2004) Diary keeping and well-being. *Proceedings of the British Psychological Society*, (1) 62.

Ellis, A and Dryden, W (1999) *The practice of rational emotive behaviour therapy*. London: Free Association Books.

Goleman, D (1996) *Emotional intelligence*. London: Bloomsbury.

Health and Safety Executive (2004) *Self-reported work-related illness in 2003/04 results from the labour force survey*. London: Health and Safety Executive.

Horner, N (2004) *What is social work? Context and perspectives*. Exeter: Learning Matters.

Linley, PA and Joseph, S (2004) *Positive psychology in practice*. Hoboken, NJ: Wiley.

Milner, J and O'Byrne, P (2002) *Assessment in social work*. Basingstoke: Palgrave.

Nicolson, P, Bayne, R and Owen, J (2006) *Applied psychology for social workers*. Basingstoke: Palgrave.

Parker, J and Bradley, G (2003) *Social work practice: Assessment, planning, intervention and review*. Exeter: Learning Matters.

Seligman, M (1998) *Learned optimism*. New York: Free Press.

Seligman, M (2003) *Authentic happiness*. London: Nicholas Brealey.

Sutton, C (2006) *Helping families with troubled children*. 2nd edition. Chichester: John Wiley.

Thompson, N (2006) *People problems*. Basingstoke: Palgrave

Chapter 5

Argyris, C and Schön, D (1996) *Organisational learning II*. Boston, MA: Addison-Wesley.

Baldwin, M (2004) Critical reflection: Opportunities and threats to professional learning and service development in social work organisations. In N Gould and M Baldwin (eds) *Social work, critical reflection and the learning organisation*. Aldershot: Ashgate.

Boud, D and Knight, S (1996) Course design and reflective practice. In N Gould and I Taylor (eds) *Reflective learning for social work*. Aldershot: Ashgate.

Department of Health (1990) *Community care in the next decade and beyond: Policy guidance*. London: The Stationery Office.

Department of Health (2007) *Putting people first: A shared vision and commitment to the transformation of adult social care*. London: Department of Health.

Department of Health (2008) *The case for change: Why England needs a new care and support system*. London: Department of Health.

Gould, N (2004) Introduction: The learning organisation and reflective practice – the emergence of a concept. In N Gould and M Baldwin (eds) *Social work, critical reflection and the learning organisation*. Aldershot: Ashgate.

Henderson, J (2001) He's not my carer – he's my husband: Personal and policy constructions of care in mental health. *Journal of Social Work Practice*, 15 (2), 149–59.

Johnsson, E and Svensson, K (2004) Theory in social work – Some reflections on understanding and explaining interventions. *European Journal of Social Work*, 8 (4), 419–33.

Lipsky, M (1980) *Street-level bureaucracy: Dilemmas of the individual in public service*. New York: Russell Sage Foundation.

Mantell, A (2006) *Huntington's disease: The carer's story*. Unpublished DPhil., University of Sussex.

Marcus, G (1998) *Ethnography through thick and thin*. New Jersey: Princetown Publications.

Morris, J (1993) *Independent lives: Community care and disabled people*. London: Macmillan.

Nolan, M (2001) The positive aspects of caring. In S Payne and C Ellis-Hill (eds) *Chronic and terminal illness: New perspectives on caring and carers*. Oxford: Oxford University Press.

Parker, R (1981) Tending and social policy. In E Goldman and S Hatch (eds) *A new look at the personal social services*. London: Policy Studies Institute.

Parker, J and Bradley, G (2010) *Social work practice: Assessment, planning, intervention and review*. 3rd edition. Exeter: Learning Matters.

Qureshi, H and Simons, K (1987) Resources within families: Caring for elderly people. In J Brannen and G Wilson (eds) *Give and take in families: Studies in resource distribution*. London: Allen & Unwin.

Schofield, H (ed.) (1998) *Family caregivers: Disability, illness and ageing*. St Leonards, NSW: Allen & Unwin.

Schön, D (1983) *How professionals think in action*. New York: Basic Books.

Thomas, C (1993) De-constructing concepts of care. *Sociology*, 27 (4), 649–69.

Trevithick, P (2005) Social work skills: A practice handbook. 2nd edition. Maidenhead: Open University Press/McGraw-Hill.

Chapter 6

Braithwaite, R (2001) *Managing aggression*. London: Routledge.

Ferguson, H (2005) Working with violence, the emotions and the psycho-social dynamics of child protection: Reflections on the Victoria Climbié case. *Social Work Education*, 24 (7), 781–95.

Ferguson, H and O'Reilly, M (2001) *Keeping children safe: Child abuse, child protection and the promotion of welfare*. Dublin: A&A Farmer.

Gould, N and Baldwin, M (2004) *Social work, critical reflection and learning organization*. Aldershot: Ashgate.

Howe, D (1995) *Attachment theory for social work practice*. Basingstoke: Palgrave.

Koprowska, J (2010) *Communication and interpersonal skills in social work*. 3rd edition. Exeter: Learning Matters.

Laming, H (2003) *The Victoria Climbié Inquiry*. London: The Stationery Office. **www.victoria-climbie-inquiry.org.uk/finreport/report.pdf**

Reder, P and Duncan, S (1999) *Lost innocents: A follow-up study of fatal child abuse*. London: Routledge.

Ruch, G (2002) From triangle to spiral: reflective practice in social work education, practice and research. *Social Work Education*, 21 (2), 199–216.

Rustin, M (2005) Conceptual analysis of critical moments in Victoria Climbié's life. *Child and Family Social Work*, 10, 11–19.

Schön, D (1991) *The reflective practitioner: How professionals think in action*. Aldershot: Ashgate.

Stanley, J and Goddard, C (2002) *In the firing line: Power and violence in child protection work*. Chichester: Wiley.

Thompson, N (2005) *Understanding social work: Preparing for practice*. 2nd edition. Basingstoke: Palgrave.

Wallis, S (2004) *Developing research-informed practice in child care social work teams*. Durham: University of Durham. Unpublished PhD Thesis.

Chapter 7

Arshad, R (1996) Building fragile bridges: educating for change. In K Cavanagh and VE Cree, (eds), *Working with Men: Feminism and Social Work*. London: Routledge.

Baginhole, B, and Cross, C (2006) 'It Never Struck Me as Female': Investigating Men's Entry into Female-dominated Occupations. *Journal of Gender Studies* 15 (1), 35–48.

Bowl, R (1985) *Changing the Nature of Masculinity: a Task for Social Work?* Norwich: University of East Anglia BASW.

Bowl, R (2001) Men and Community Care. In A. Christie (ed.) *Men in Social Work*. Basingstoke: Palgrave.

Calhoun, C (1992) Emotion Work. In E.B.Cole and S.Coultrap-Quinn (eds) *Exploration In Feminist Ethics,Theory and Practice*. Bloomington, IN: Indiana University.

Christie, A (1998) Is Social Work a Non-traditional Occupation for Men?, *British Journal of Social Work* 28, 491–510.

Christie, A (2001) Gendered Discourses of Welfare, Men and Social Work. In A. Christie (ed.) *Men in Social Work*. Basingstoke: Palgrave.

Chusmir, LC (1990) Men who make nontraditional career choices, *Journal of Counselling and Development* 69, 11–16.

Clare, A (2000) *On Men: Masculinity in Crisis*. London: Chatto & Windus.

Collier, R (1998) *Masculinities, Crime and Criminology: Men, Heterosexuality and the Criminal(ised) Other*. London: Sage.

Connell, RW (1987) *Masculinities*. Cambridge: Polity.

Cree, V (1996) Why Do Men Care? In K.Cavanagh and VE Cree (eds), *Working with Men: Feminism and Social Work*. London: Routledge.

Cree, V (2001) Men and Masculinities in Social Work Education. In A Christie (ed) *Men and Social Work*. Basingstoke: Palgrave.

Dale, J and Foster, P (1986) *Feminists and State Welfare*. London: Routledge and Kegan Paul.

Dalley, G (1996) *Ideologies of Caring*. London: Macmillan.

Duncombe, J and Marsden, D (1993) Love and intimacy: The gender division of emotion and emotion work. *Sociology* 27, 221–41.

Duncombe, J and Marsden, D (1998) 'Stepford wives' and hollow men? Doing emotion work, doing gender and 'authenticity'. In intimate heterosxual relationships. In G Bendelow and SJ Williams (eds) *Emotions in Social Life: Critical Themes and Contemporary Issues.* London: Routledge.

Faludi, S (1999) *Stiffed: The Betrayal of the Modern Man*. London: Chatto & Windus.

Ferguson, H (2005) Working with Violence, the Emotions and the Psycho-social Dynamics of Child Protection: Reflections on the Victoria Climbie Case. *Social Work Education* 24 (7), 781–95.

Flam, H (2002) Corporate emotions and emotions in corporations. In Barbalet, J (ed) *Emotions and Sociology*. Oxford: Blackwell Publishing.

Gaine, C (2001) If it's not hurting it's not working: teaching teachers about 'race'. *Research Papers in Education* 16 (1), 93–113.

Gorman, H and Postle, K (2003) *Transforming Community Care: A Distorted Vision.* Birmingham: Venture Press.

Gough, B (2001) Biting Your Tongue: negotiating masculinities in contemporary Britain. *Journal of Gender Studies* 10 (2), 169–85.

Halsey, AH (1993) *Guardian* 23 February.

Hearn, J (2001) Men, Social Work and Men's Violence to Women. In A Christie (ed) *Men in Social Work*. Basingstoke: Palgrave.

Hicks, S (2001) Men Social Workers in Children's Services: 'Will the Real Man Please Stand Up?' In A Christie (ed) *Men in Social Work*. Basingstoke: Palgrave.

Hochschild, A (1983) *The Managed Heart: Commercialization of Human Feeling.* Berkeley, CA: University of California Press.

Kerfoot, D (2001) The Organization of Intimacy: Managerialism, Masculinity and the Masculine Subject. In SM Whitehead and FJ Barrett (eds) *The Masculinities Reader.* London: Cambridge Press.

Kimmel, M (1990) After fifteen years: the impact of the sociology of masculinity on the sociology of masculinity. In J Hearn and D Morgan (eds), *Men, Masculinities and Social Theory*. London: Unwin Hyman.

Kumar, K (1995) *From Post-Industrial to Post-Modern Society*. Oxford: Basil Blackwell.

MacInnes, J (1998) *The End of Masculinity.* Buckingham: Open University Press.

McLean, J (2003) Men as Minority: Men Employed in Statutory Social Care Workforce. *Journal of Social Work* 3 (1), 45–68.

Perry, RW, and Cree, VE (2003) The changing gender profile of applicants to qualifying social work training in the UK. *Social Work Education* 22 (4), 377–83.

Pringle, K (2001) Men in Social Work:The Double Edge. In A Christie (ed) *Men and Social Work.* Basingstoke: Palgrave.

Seidler, VJ (1994) *Unreasonable Men: Masculinity and Social Theory.* London: Routledge.

Seidler, VJ (1998) Masculinity, violence and emotional life. In G Bendelow and SJ Williams (eds) *Emotions in Social Life: Critical Themes and Contemporary Issues.* London: Routledge.

Scourfield, J (2002) Reflections on Gender, Knowledge and Values in Social Work. *British Journal of Social Work* 32, 1–15.

Scourfield, J (2003) *Gender and Child Protection.* Basingstoke: Palgrave.

Simpson, R (2004) Masculinity at work; the experiences of men in female dominated professions. *Work, Employment and society* 18 (2), 349–68.

Smith, M (2005) *Surviving Fears in Health and Social Care; The Terrors of Night and the Arrows of Day.* London: Jessica Kingsley Publishers.

Tannen, D (1997) *Working nine to five.* London: Virago.

Telford, L (1996) Selves in Bunkers. In C Cheng (ed.) *Masculinities in Organizations.* London: SAGE.

Thompson, N, Stradling, S, Murphy, M, and O'Neill, P (1996) Stress and Organizational Culture. *British Journal of Social Work* 26, 647–65.

Williams, C (1993) Introduction. In C Williams (ed) *Doing 'Women's Work': Men in Nontraditional Occupations.* London: Sage Publications.

Williams, C (1995) *Still a Man's World: Men Who Do Women's Work.* Berkeley, CA: University of California Press.

Chapter 8

Adams, R, Dominelli, L and Payne, M (2000) *Social work themes, issues and critical debates.* 2nd edition. Basingstoke: Palgrave.

Bolton, G (2005) *Reflective practice: Writing and professional development.* 2nd edition. London: Sage.

Boud, D, Keogh, R and Walker, D (eds) (1985) *Reflection: Turning experience into learning.* London: Kogan Page.

Cottrell, S (2003) *The study skills handbook.* 2nd edition. Basingstoke: Palgrave Macmillan.

Department of Health (2002) *Requirements for social work training.* London: The Stationery Office.

Department of Health (2004) *Every Child Matters* London: The Stationery Office.

Department of Health (2006) *Our health, our care, our say.* London: The Stationery Office.

Edwards, C (2003) The involvement of service users in the assessment of service users in the assessment of Diploma in Social Work students on practice placements. *Social Work Education*, 22 (4), 341–9.

Fook, J (2002) *Social work: Critical theory and practice.* London: Sage.

Ixer, G (1999) There's no such thing as reflection. *British Journal of Social Work*, 29 (4), 513–27.

Lam, C, Wong, H and Leung, T (2007) *British Journal of Social Work*, 37 (1), 91–105.

Parker, J (2004) *Effective practice learning in social work.* Exeter: Learning Matters.

Schön, D (1983) *The reflective practitioner: How professionals think in action.* London: Temple Smith.

Schön, D (1986) *Educating the reflective practitioner.* Oxford: Jossey-Bass.

SCIE (2003) *A framework for supporting and assessing practice learning.* SCIE position paper 2.

Thompson, N (2000) *Understanding social work*. Basingstoke: Macmillan.

Watson, D and West, J (2006) *Social work process and practice*. Basingstoke: Palgrave.

Chapter 9

Alston, M and Bowles, W (2003) *Research for social workers: An introduction to methods*. 2nd edition. London: Routledge.

Chartered Institute of Training and Development (2004) *Training and development, survey report*. **www.cipd.co.uk**. Accessed 25 October 2006.

Cunningham, G (2004) Supervision and governance. In D Statham (ed) *Managing front line practice in social care*. London: Jessica Kingsley Publishers.

Darvill, G (1997) *The management of work-based learning, a guide for managers of social care and social work on raising standards of practice*. London: The Stationery Office.

Eraut, M (2001) Learning challenges for knowledge-based organisations. In J Stevens (ed) *Workplace learning in europe*. London: Chartered Institute of Personnel and Development (CIPD).

Gould, N (1996) Introduction: Social work education and the crisis of the professions. In N Gould and I Taylor (eds) *Reflective learning for social work*. Aldershot: Arena.

Gould, N and Baldwin, M (2004) *Social work, critical reflection and the learning organization*. Aldershot: Ashgate.

Henderson, J and Seden, J (2003) What do we want from social care managers? Aspirations and realities. In J Reynolds, J Henderson, J Seden, J Charlesworth and A Bullman (eds) *The managing care reader*. London: Routledge and the Open University.

Ixer, G (1999) There's no such thing as reflection. *British Journal of Social Work*, 29(4), 513–27.

Kearney, P (ed) (1999) *Managing practice project report*. London: National Institute for Social Work.

Kearney, P (2004) First line managers, the mediator of standards and quality of practice. In D Statham (ed) *Managing front line practice in social care*. London: Jessica Kingsley Publishers .

Morrison, T (1993) *Staff supervision in social care: an action learning approach*. Brighton: Pavilion Publishing.

Rosen, G (ed) (2000) *Integrity, the organisation and the first-line manager, discussion papers*. London: National Institute for Social Work.

Sawdon, C and Sawdon, D (1995) The supervision partnership: a whole greater than the sum of its parts. In J Pritchard (ed) *Good practice in supervision*. London: Jessical Kingsley Publishers.

Schein, EH (1987) *Process consultation, volume 11: lessons for managers and consultants*. Reading, MA: Addison-Wesley.

Senge, PM (2006) *The fifth discipline: the art and practice of learning organization*, London: Doubleday.

Statham, D (ed) (2004) *Managing front line practice in social care*. London: Jessica Kingsley Publishers.

Thompson, N (2000) *Understanding social work: preparing for practice*. Basingstoke: Macmillan.

Chapter 10

Anderson, NR and West, MA (1998) Measuring the climate for work group innovation: development and validation of the team climate inventory. *Journal of Organisational Behaviour*, 19, 235–8.

Ansari, W and Phillips, CJ (2001) Partnerships, community participation and intersectoral collaboration in South Africa. *Journal of Interprofessional Care*. 15 (2), 119–32.

Avery, GC (2004) *Understanding leadership*. London: Sage.

Bate, P (1994) *Strategies for cultural change*. Oxford: Butterworth-Heinemann.

Biggs, S (1997) Interprofessional collaboration: Problems and prospects. In J Ovretveit, P Mathias and T Thompson (eds) *Interprofessional working for health and social care*. Basingstoke: Macmillan.

Biggs, J (1999) *Teaching for quality learning at university*. Buckingham: Open University Press.

Bulman, C and Shutz, S (2004) *Reflective practice in nursing*. Oxford: Blackwell.

Burns, JM (1978) *Leadership*. New York: Harper and Row.

Department of Health (2004) *Every Child Matters*. London: Department of Health.

Department of Health (2004) *Independence, well being and choice*. London: Department of Health.

Department of Health (2006) *Transition: Getting it right for young people: Improving the transition of young people with long-term conditions*. London: Department of Health.

Department of Health (2007) *Putting People First*. London: Department of Health.

Department of Health (2008) *High quality care for all*. NHS next stage review, final report. Norwich: The Stationery Office.

Gouva, M, Mantzoukas, S, Mitona, E and Damigos, D (2009) Understanding nurses' psychosomatic complications that relate to the practice of nursing. *Nursing and Health Sciences*, 11 (2), 154–9.

Gray, B (1989) *Collaborating finding common ground for multiparty problems*. San Francisco, CA: Jossey-Bass.

Hackett, M and Spurgeon, P (1998) Developing our leaders in the future. *Health Manpower Management*, 24 (5), 170–7.

Hudson, B (1999) Primary health care and social care: Working across professional boundaries. *Managing Community Care*, 7 (1), 15–22.

Jasper, M (2005) The challenges of healthcare leadership in Britain today. In M Jasper, and M Jumaa (eds) *Effective healthcare leadership*. Oxford: Blackwell.

Kanter, RM (1994) Collaborative advantage: the art of alliances. *Harvard Business Review*, July–August, 96–108.

Loxley, A (1997) *Collaboration in health and welfare: working with difference*. London: Jessica Kingsley Publishers.

McCray, J (2003a) *Towards a conceptual framework for interprofessional practice in the field of learning disability*. PhD Thesis. Department of Social Work studies, University of Southampton.

McCray, J (2003b) Leading interprofessional practice: A conceptual framework to support practitioners in the field of learning disability. *Journal of Nursing Management*, 11, 387–95.

McCray, J (2006) Nursing practice in an interprofessional context. In R Hogston and B Marjoram (eds) *Foundations of nursing practice leading the way*. Basingstoke: Palgrave.

Odegard, A and Strype, J (2009) Perceptions of interprofessional collaboration within child mental health care in Norway. *Journal of Interprofessional Care*, 23 (3), 286–96.

Percy Smith, J (2005) *What works in strategic partnerships for children?* Essex: Barnardos.

Pollard, K, Sellman, D and Senior, B (2005) The need for interprofessional working. In G Barrett, D Sellman and J Thomas (eds) *Interprofessional working in health and social care*. Basingstoke: Palgrave.

Quinney, A (2006) *Collaborative social work practice*. Exeter: Learning Matters.

Schön, DA (1983) *The reflective practitioner: How professionals think in action*. London: Temple South.

Taylor, I, Sharland, E, Sebba, J, Leviche, P, Keep, E and Orr, D (2006) *The learning, teaching and assessment of partnership work in social work education*. Policy Press: Bristol.

Index

Transforming Social Work Practice – titles in the series

To order, please contact our distributor BEBC Distribution, Albion Close, Parkstone, Poole, BH12 3LL.
Telephone 0845 230 9000, email **learningmatters@bebc.co.uk**. You can also find more information on
each of these titles and our other learning resources at **www.learningmatters.co.uk**.